A Leadership Journey of Discovery

Written by: Rick Regueira

ISBN 979-8-9934871-0-6 (Paperback)
First Edition, 2025
Published by **TE Publishing House**
Printed by **Amazon KDP**

This work reflects the author's experiences and opinions. Some details have been adapted to protect privacy.

All trademarks, logos, and brand names are the property of their respective owners and are used for identification purposes only.

For more information about this book, speaking engagements, or upcoming events, visit:
www.teculture.com/a-leadership-journey-of-discovery

Dedication

This book reflects the collective effort of many remarkable individuals. A transformation of this scale is never the work of one person alone, but of a community bound by courage, collaboration, and belief in what's possible.

I want to honor those who played central roles in shaping this journey: George Labelle, Tony Ronconi, Bob Sarnack, Christina Alonso, and the entire IPC Agile Team. They were the true heroes behind the scenes, driving value, demonstrating ownership, and embodying the principles that redefined our culture.

To the community members who helped expand Agile learning beyond our walls, thank you for your passion and commitment to sharing knowledge and inspiring others.

To Regina and our family, thank you for your patience, love, and belief in me throughout this journey. Your support gave me strength during the hardest times and joy in every accomplishment. To my mother, siblings, and children, thank you for your unconditional love and the values that shaped who I am today.

This book is also dedicated to every team, leader, and coach who continues the work of transforming organizations through empathy, trust, and purpose. You are the heart of this movement.

Contents

This journey has been **full of peaks and valleys.** Each step has shaped not just my career, but also **who I am as a person.**

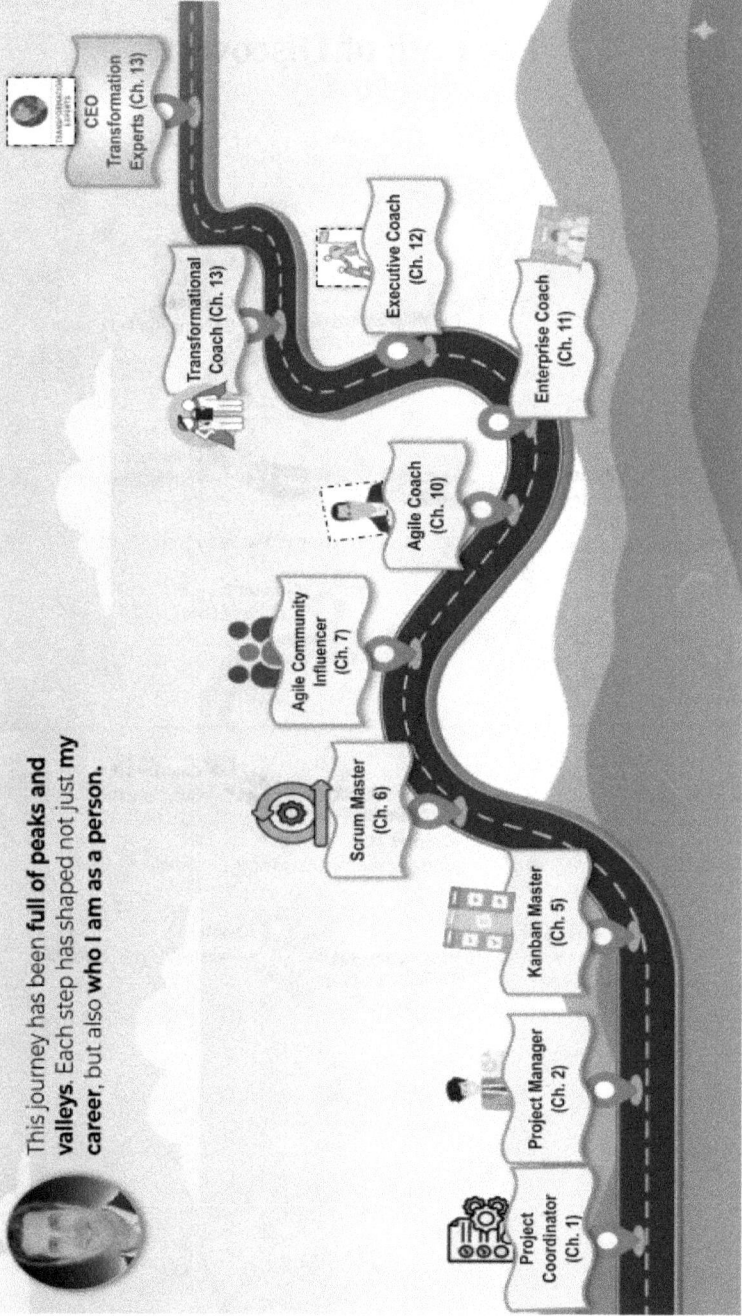

Project Coordinator (Ch. 1)

Project Manager (Ch. 2)

Kanban Master (Ch. 5)

Scrum Master (Ch. 6)

Agile Community Influencer (Ch. 7)

Agile Coach (Ch. 10)

Enterprise Coach (Ch. 11)

Executive Coach (Ch. 12)

Transformational Coach (Ch. 13)

CEO Transformation Experts (Ch. 13)

The Path of Discovery

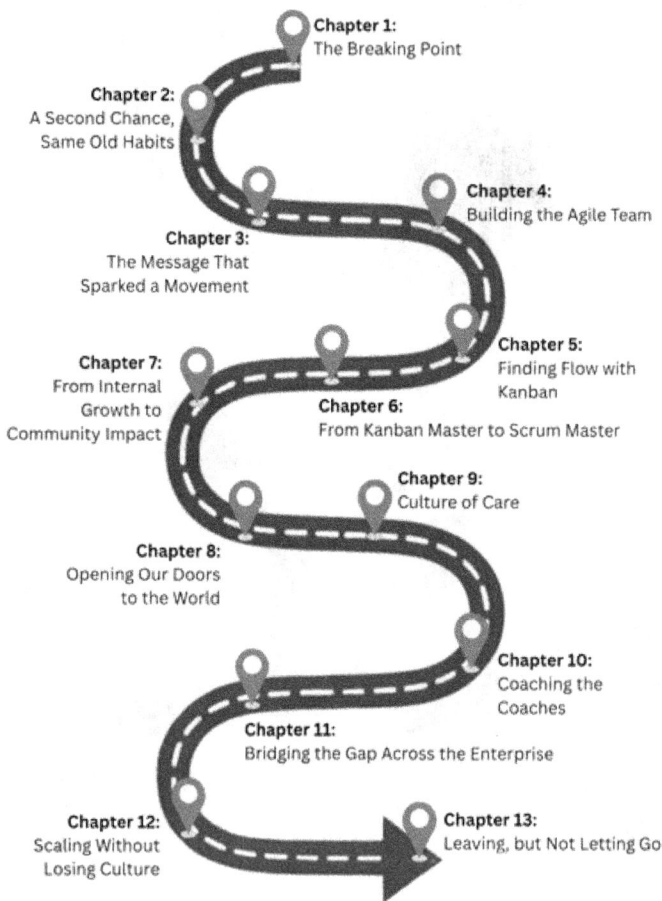

Chapter 1:
The Breaking Point

Chapter 2:
A Second Chance,
Same Old Habits

Chapter 4:
Building the Agile Team

Chapter 3:
The Message That
Sparked a Movement

Chapter 5:
Finding Flow with
Kanban

Chapter 7:
From Internal
Growth to
Community Impact

Chapter 6:
From Kanban Master to Scrum Master

Chapter 9:
Culture of Care

Chapter 8:
Opening Our Doors
to the World

Chapter 10:
Coaching the
Coaches

Chapter 11:
Bridging the Gap Across the Enterprise

Chapter 12:
Scaling Without
Losing Culture

Chapter 13:
Leaving, but Not Letting Go

Foreword:

by George Labelle, CIO (Retired), IPC

"If you are a technology executive, a manager, or an engineer, my story may sound familiar. For years, we struggled with projects that were late, over budget, or misaligned with what the business truly needed. The frustration was real, and the risks were high.

When Agile entered the picture, it offered the possibility of a new way forward. But what made the real difference for us at IPC was not only the adoption of new practices, but the leadership and guidance of Rick Regueira.

Rick wasn't just a coach for our teams; he was also my coach. He had an uncommon ability to know when I was pushing too hard and when I needed to push harder. More importantly, he brought a human dimension into what could have easily become a purely mechanical change effort.

That is what this book captures. It is not only the story of Agile at IPC, but the story of how transformation takes hold when leadership, courage, and connection meet. In these pages, you will find the lessons, challenges, and breakthroughs that shaped our journey, told through Rick's perspective.

So, settle in. You are about to walk alongside Rick through the highs and lows of a transformation that changed a company, a culture, and a life."

George Labelle.

Prologue:

When Success Hides the Struggle

This journey of leadership discovery didn't just change how I worked. It reshaped who I was, at a time when everything looked fine on the outside but was falling apart on the inside.

There was a time when I was burning out quietly. To the outside world, I looked like I was succeeding. I was managing multi-million-dollar projects, delivering results, and climbing the corporate ladder. But inside, I was tense, disconnected, and losing sight of the kind of leader and person I wanted to be.

This is not a book about frameworks or tools. It's about a journey of rediscovering purpose, reconnecting with people, and learning how to lead with empathy in a world that often rewards control. It's the story of how one transformation, at just the right moment, opened the door to a new way of leading and a new way of living.

Chapter 1:

The Breaking Point:
When Control
Masqueraded as Leadership

Sometimes, what looks like leadership is really just fear in disguise. My parents were raised in Cuba and fled communist rule without speaking English. With four young children, they boarded a plane and left everything behind. Under communism, your voice, your concerns, even your pain are silenced. My parents gave up the familiar streets they knew, their close-knit community, and the family they loved so their children could grow up with freedom and opportunity. **Figure 1.1** shows those early days of rebuilding in the United States, a reminder of both the difficulty and the hope that defined their start. They taught me to lead with respect, kindness, and empathy. Somewhere along the way, I buried that part of myself under deadlines and deliverables.

Figure 1.1: Can you guess who I am in this picture?

My career as a leader began in the demanding world of IT project management. I had over eight years of experience managing large-scale initiatives for enterprise companies. What drew me in was the idea that behind every moon landing or skyscraper, someone was quietly steering the ship. It was a career built on guiding progress from behind the scenes.

Becoming a senior Project Manager wasn't easy. I started as a project coordinator, responsible for small efforts. After four years, I qualified to take the Project Management Professional (PMP) exam. Passing opened the door to larger, more complex assignments. A few years later, I moved into the Senior Project Manager role. See me dressed like a PiMP in **Figure 1.2.**

Figure 1.2: Because every PMP needs a little flair.

I had made it. I was running multi-million-dollar projects with pressure to deliver results on time and within budget. No excuses. I led with confidence, but not always with pride. There was a stretch when I barely recognized the person staring back at me.

One of my former bosses used to say, "You're large and in charge." That mantra became my marching orders. It reinforced what I believed: dominate the room, control the plan, never show weakness. We were rewarded for being tough, for pushing hard, for enforcing deadlines without flinching. That's what success looked like, or so I thought.

And I was good at it. I was praised for being in control, promoted for hitting deadlines, and recognized for pushing teams to deliver. But beneath the surface, the stress was constant. My eyelid twitched under pressure, a quiet protest from a body I ignored. Still, I pressed on, convinced that's what leaders did.

I didn't just pass on pressure, I dismissed emotion. I treated it like static instead of information worth hearing. I focused on numbers, dates, and checklists, not people. I thought leadership meant keeping everything moving, no matter the cost. Feelings were distractions. Vulnerability was weakness. That mindset carried a cost I would one day be forced to pay.

The moment of reckoning came unexpectedly. It started as a routine PMO status update and ended as a mirror I could not avoid.

Our project had slipped from green to yellow. That triggered a deep need to reassert control. Requirements were behind, so I pulled the business analyst aside. I asked why the work was delayed, but in truth, I wasn't listening. I just wanted the work done faster, even if it meant asking her to stay late.

She didn't argue. She didn't resist. She just stood there. And then her eyes filled with tears. She walked away quietly. But the moment stayed with me.

That story still makes me pause. Not because it was the first time I pushed too hard, but because it was the first time I realized I had crossed a line. I wasn't leading. I was bullying. And worse, I had mistaken that behavior for effectiveness. That realization cracked something in me.

She had trusted me with her challenges, and I failed to give her respect. I didn't truly listen. To this day, I don't know what support she needed, but I know I didn't offer it. In truth, I felt embarrassed and avoided confronting her again. That silence became its own lesson, showing me how fear of facing my mistakes kept me from repairing trust.

That incident at work didn't just sting; it awakened a memory buried deep. The shift from that quiet moment of tears to a childhood lesson may seem unlikely, but both carried the same truth: leadership is about service, not control. I was thirteen and late for a basketball game. On the way, my mom stopped the car to give our neighbor a ride to work.

I cried in the back seat, angry and confused. Why would she choose someone else over me? Years later, I understood. It wasn't about the ride; it was about character. She was teaching me that service sometimes means setting aside your own urgency. That memory lingered as I grew older and recalling it after the analyst incident helped me realize how far I had drifted from those values.

That lesson, rooted in who I was, had been buried under the armor I thought leadership required. Remembering my mom's quiet act of service prepared me for the next part of my story, the moment when the weight of my personal life came crashing down.
When things go wrong, they rarely go wrong alone. Around that same time, my personal life collapsed. I was going through a painful separation and had to leave my home, which meant less time with my children. My property investments, meant to secure my family's future, defaulted during the 2008 housing crisis, wiping out my savings. At work, I was on the verge of losing my job, yet I carried the weight silently, unwilling to ask for help.

One night I arrived home exhausted and light-headed, my chest tight with pain. Fear swept over me. Was this something serious? I called my sister Ale, a nurse married to a doctor, and the urgency in her voice when she told me to get to the ER made my stomach drop. In the hospital, they suspected a heart attack, then a rare virus. They ran every test imaginable, even threading a catheter to my heart. Nothing. The night before, I had gone dancing and drank too much cranberry juice. I half-joked that maybe that was to blame. But deep down, I knew better.

The truth was I was unraveling. My marriage, my finances, my career, all of it was crumbling. I felt ashamed, isolated, terrified of letting anyone see how broken I was. Lying in that hospital bed, it felt almost like a dream. I couldn't believe this was happening to me. I had always taken care of my health so carefully. So what was I doing here? All I wanted was to get out. I was grateful for how much my family cared for me, yet in that moment I even questioned why I had called them. That inner conflict showed just how disoriented I was. When the doctors finally stepped back with no clear answers, I felt relief mixed with confusion. I wanted to believe I was fine, but deep down I knew something had to change. Looking back, I know what the real culprit was: stress. It had eroded me from the inside out, leaving my body sounding alarms I refused to hear.

That hospital stay became a turning point, leading directly into deeper questions about who I was becoming as a leader and as a person. It was no longer just about surviving the projects or the pressure; it was about redefining the kind of leader and human being I wanted to be.

The worst part wasn't how others saw me. It was how I saw myself. That day with the business analyst marked the first crack in the hardened identity I had spent years building. Looking back, it was also the beginning of a transformation I didn't yet know I needed.

The problem wasn't just the pressure or the culture; it was not knowing other ways existed. Ignorance kept me orthodox.

Project management itself wasn't the enemy. It is a powerful discipline with tools designed to bring structure, clarity, and predictability to complex initiatives. But applied through a control-driven mindset, those tools can create silos, reduce collaboration, and put process over people. The problem wasn't project management, it was how we were using it
.

I thought I was doing what good leaders did. I had no models of leadership that prioritized empathy or collaboration. I was trapped in a system that valued control over connection, urgency over understanding. Without a different framework, I kept repeating what I had been taught. And when your work no longer aligns with who you are, something eventually breaks.

For me, that break began with a truth I could no longer deny: my so-called leadership was hurting people. I didn't know it yet, but a new job at a new company would quietly open the door to a different kind of leadership, one where connection, not control, set the pace.

And to be clear: I believe the chain of incidents truly began that day, the day she cried.

Key Learnings from Chapter 1

- Leadership without empathy is just control. True leadership begins with listening.
- Stress ignored will eventually surface. Hiding your struggles doesn't make you stronger, it makes you fragile.
- Silence after a mistake can do as much damage as the mistake itself. Repairing trust begins with courage to face it.
- One painful moment, whether in the office or in a hospital bed, can become the wake-up call that sparks transformation.

I once believed leadership was about holding the line. Now I understand that real leadership begins when we let go of control, of ego, and of the illusion that we must have all the answers. The first crack in my identity didn't destroy me, it set me free. That moment of reckoning marked the start of a journey of unlearning and rediscovery. What I needed next wasn't another title or another project. What I needed was a second chance, and it was waiting for me just down the hall, with a new team and a new way of working I didn't even know existed.

Chapter 2:

A Second Chance, Same Old Habits

S ometimes your old habits show up before you even unpack your boxes.

The job hunt had been brutal. Endless applications, late-night resume edits, and that constant loop of hope and rejection. Then, one afternoon, everything changed. I got the call. A new door had opened, and I was invited to interview at IPC (Independent Purchasing Cooperative for Subway). Do you know that moment when your stomach flips because opportunity might finally be knocking? That was me. After months underwater, I was finally coming up for air (**Figure 2.1**).

Figure 2.1: Exploring the depths of the job market.

As I prepared for the interview, I started my research, I was instantly drawn in. Subway was everywhere, but IPC was the powerhouse behind the scenes, supporting thousands of franchisees. Their mission to help others succeed hit home.

Then I read about Fred DeLuca, Subway's founder. One young man, one sandwich shop, one unstoppable dream. He didn't wait for the perfect timing; he created it. His story of grit inspired me to want to understand the secret sauce (**See Figure 2.2** the picture of me meeting **Fred DeLuca** for the first time).

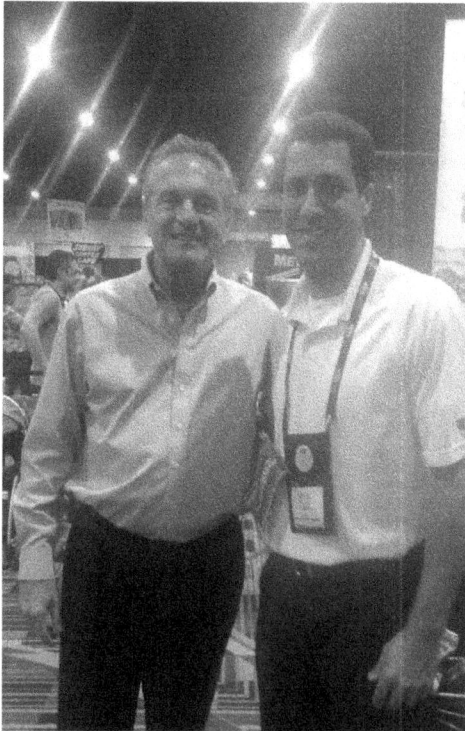

Figure 2.2: Honored to have met Fred DeLuca

Coaching Guidance:

Opportunity doesn't wait. It rewards the ready. I tell my kids this all the time: prepare before the moment arrives. After college, I was a standby player for a basketball team touring Colombia with the Harlem Globetrotters. For weeks, I practiced, unsure if I would ever get on that plane. Then Hurricane Andrew hit. Flights were canceled left and right, but somehow ours stayed on schedule.

At the airport, I clutched my passport, something I had applied for years earlier just in case. Some teammates couldn't go because the customs office was closed. But I was ready. That one small act of foresight turned into an unforgettable adventure: roaring crowds, autographs, and meeting the legendary Meadowlark Lemon. That moment stuck with me: preparation turns chance into choice.

I suited up and made sure I was there early. My interview was with Tony Ronconi, Director of IT Infrastructure and Support. His handshake was firm, his energy focused. We started by talking process and delivery, but when the topic turned to family, something shifted. We shared stories about parenting and laughed about the daily chaos of raising kids. The atmosphere lightened, and for the first time in a long time, I saw leadership in its purest form: connection built on empathy.

Tony had that rare balance of strength and warmth, the kind of leader who didn't need to shout to command respect. I left the room thinking, this is the kind of leader I want to be. It stopped being about getting the job. It became about learning to lead with head and heart.

When I joined IPC in 2010, it felt like walking into a high-performing orchestra. Everyone looked sharp, the halls were spotless, and the vibe in the building was focused and professional. No clients ever visited, but professionalism was part of the culture. It was who they were.

The organization was smaller than those I'd worked in before, with a strong family-oriented vibe and a sense of personal ownership that ran deep. Many of the executives were original founders who still walked the halls. The people were warm, the environment was kind, and on paper, it looked like the perfect place to reset.

But if I'm honest, I didn't reset, I simply relocated. I told myself I just needed to ramp up, work harder, stay sharp, prove myself.

Starting a new job always comes with a mix of excitement and pressure. You want to learn quickly, understand what's expected of you, and pick up the organization's norms. Every time I've started a new role, I've pushed myself to dedicate an extra two hours each day, on top of the regular workday, for about three months. That time is focused on learning the tools, systems, people, and processes I need to succeed.

I've found that creating a structured work environment helps me perform better. I use templates and repeatable systems to simplify my workflow. I'm not someone who can memorize everything and recall it on the spot. I need to execute in order to retain. I am not afraid of hard work. My learning strategy is to look for patterns, frameworks I can reuse, which make learning faster and more intuitive.

When I joined IPC, the organization was still working in a traditional project management style, much like most companies at the time. That style had deep roots in a system designed for a very different kind of work.

The Waterfall approach was born during the early 20th century, gaining prominence in the Industrial Revolution. Its purpose was clear: to produce the same product, like a car, faster, cheaper, and with fewer errors. It thrived in environments where the end goal was well-defined and unchanging.

The focus was on creating the "perfect plan." As a Project Manager who had worked extensively with traditional methodologies, I was used to buffering both time and cost estimates to prepare for variances. In my experience, those initial project estimates were rarely accurate, and padding timelines was a common way to mitigate risk and stay on track.

Work was structured into linear phases, each managed by a specialist. The focus was efficiency. Workers weren't asked to solve problems or innovate; they were expected to follow instructions and execute tasks with precision. Managers oversaw the process to ensure consistency and compliance. It was a system designed for predictability, not adaptability.

It didn't take long for my old habits to surface. Even though my badge had changed, the same old symptoms returned: long hours, disconnected teams, missed deadlines, and low morale.

One of my first projects was to replace the corporate firewall with a new system, a physical device that protects internal computer systems from external hackers. The project was complex, and while our initial plan was solid and thoughtfully constructed, it lacked input from all the necessary departments and had never been fully tested. In project management, you're often not the expert in the technology, you rely on your team for that. But since this team was new to me, and I didn't yet have a history of their successes or failures, it was hard to judge the reliability of the plan. Some managers were pushing to move quickly. I was new to IPC, still finding my place, and I knew I didn't have much clout. I felt the pressure to execute, even though I had concerns.

But the biggest issue wasn't just technical risk, it was that we hadn't brought the right departments together to align and plan as a unified team. There was no synergy across the silos. Had we coordinated better upfront, we could have supported each other through the complexity instead of reacting to it alone. I remember feeling torn, do I protect the process, or protect my role? That sense of isolation was crushing.

Thankfully, my boss, the PMO manager, escalated the risks on my behalf. Without that intervention, the team would have gone ahead with the switch. It was one of the first moments where I realized leadership didn't always mean going it alone. Sometimes, it meant leaning on others who could see what you couldn't.

Looking back, that firewall project was a turning point. It reminded me how easy it was to fall into old habits, even in a new place. I hadn't truly started over. My surroundings had changed, but I hadn't. I was still carrying the same mindset, using the same tools, and expecting different results. I thought I had turned the page, but I had only carried the same story into a new chapter. Change wasn't just overdue; it was becoming unavoidable.

Over time, I realized that addressing complexity with more detailed planning wasn't the answer. Complexity demands something different. It requires experimentation, innovation, and continuous learning. The unknowns can't always be solved upfront. Instead, they're uncovered through doing, adjusting, and improving as we go.

Modern challenges are complex, fast-moving, and often ambiguous. We can't rely on fixed blueprints anymore. Instead of task-doers, we need problem-solvers. Today's organizations depend on knowledge workers, creative, collaborative thinkers who can navigate uncertainty and co-create solutions across systems.

IPC and most companies were still operating with a traditional delivery model, like an assembly line, where each department handed work off to the next: planning, design, development, testing, delivery. The problem? Every handoff introduced risk. Teams weren't talking to each other. Priorities shifted without warning. We kept redoing work we thought was complete. No one had a clear view of the full project, nor did anyone truly own it.

And yet, this was the norm. Most of us thought, "This is just how work works." You stop asking questions. But deep down, we knew something wasn't right. We could do better, we just didn't know how.

Still, IPC was different. It wasn't toxic. It was filled with smart, committed people who genuinely cared and wanted to improve. The foundation was strong. It just needed focus and alignment.

That's why culture eats strategy for breakfast, lunch, and dinner. In a world where no single plan survives first contact with reality, how people work together matters more than any process chart.

Key Learnings from Chapter 2

- A new environment won't fix old patterns. Lasting change requires a shift in mindset.
- Pressure and process alone cannot sustain teams. Connection and collaboration are what hold them together.
- Culture isn't just how things look on the outside, it's revealed in daily behaviors and choices.
- The first step toward transformation is recognizing when your methods no longer fit your environment.

I thought changing companies would be enough. But change doesn't happen just because your title does. I was still carrying the mindset that got results, but also left people behind. What I didn't realize yet was that leadership wasn't about having control; it was about creating connection. And until I let go of the habits that once defined me, I'd never grow into the kind of leader my teams, and my family, deserved.

What I didn't know yet was that everything was about to change.

Chapter 3:

The Message That Sparked a Movement

One message, and the room was never the same. IPC's transformation didn't start with a framework or a process, it started with a leader brave enough to question the very system he helped create.

Our CIO, George Labelle, was more than just a technology leader. He was also a permanent deacon in the Roman Catholic Church, which gave him a sense of calm and groundedness that was rare in corporate settings. You could feel it in the way he listened, the way he asked questions, and the way he carried himself. There was a depth to him, a quiet conviction, that made you pause and pay attention. He didn't need to raise his voice to command a room. His presence did that on its own.

Just a few months after I joined, he made a game-changing announcement: "We're going Agile." The picture in **Figure 3.1** captures George's expression making the announcement.

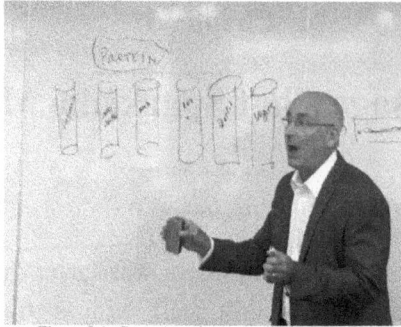

Figure 3.1: George serving up Agile for breakfast

George later shared that the decision took root during a flight back from San Francisco. He had been reading a book titled *Succeeding with Agile* by Mike Cohn, and by the time he landed, he knew something had to change. That flight, and that book, became the catalyst for a transformation that would redefine our culture. He said it plainly and firmly. "Because the way we're working isn't working. We're not delivering. We're not meeting the business needs. And we need to change. Starting now."

The room went quiet. I looked around at my coworkers to see if they were as surprised as I was, everyone wore the same bewildered expression. This wasn't a suggestion. It wasn't a brainstorming session. It was a turning point. George wasn't just announcing a new process, he was calling for a fundamental shift. You could feel it. And while most of us didn't fully understand what Agile meant, we understood the gravity of his tone. It wasn't another corporate initiative that would fade in a few months. This was different.

Still, the uncertainty stirred reactions across the company. People nodded politely, then rushed back to their desks to Google, "What is Agile?" Some were curious. Others were anxious. A few quietly updated their résumés just in case.

Hallway conversations buzzed with questions: Are we getting rid of Project Managers? Will we still have deadlines? Is this just another trend?

In the PMO team, we couldn't absorb the Agile books fast enough, so we started a book club to share our learnings. Each Project Manager picked a chapter to read and then brought their takeaways to the group. My most memorable chapter to present was on writing good user stories. In short, think of user stories as requirements that need to be completed for the project, but with a twist. The user story format didn't just capture what was needed, it also captured why. That was new for us. We were used to receiving lists of requests without context. But now, understanding the 'why' behind the request helped us ask better questions, uncover hidden needs, and connect with the real value of the work.

It reminded me of being a father to three amazing kids, Ricky, Juni, and Alex. There were so many moments I'd ask them to do something, and they'd reply, "Why?" At the time, I found it frustrating. But now I see the wisdom in their curiosity. As a parent, I wasn't exactly following the Agile user story format. The 'why' matters. It opens dialogue, builds understanding, and helps everyone move forward with clarity.

We were hungry for understanding, and this gave us a way to make sense of what was coming and support each other through it.

Then came the real wake-up call, a mandatory, two-day Agile training for the entire technology group. No laptops. No devices. Just full attention.

As we dove into the training, the most surprising part wasn't the terminology or the practices, it was that Agile started with values and principles. Ideas like prioritizing individuals and interactions over processes and tools, focusing on delivering value iteratively, and embracing change when dealing with complexity. Up until that point, most of the training I had received was grounded in best practices, documented procedures, and structured processes. But here we were, being asked to rethink the very foundation of how we worked, from the inside out. It reminded me of times when I faced complex challenges that couldn't be solved by following a checklist. It was the conversations, experiments, and small wins that got us through. That's what Agile invited us to do, face the unknown with curiosity and courage.

What struck me even more was how deeply different this was from what I had known. Traditional project management promoted silos, teams working in isolation, optimizing their own piece of the puzzle without understanding how it fit into the whole. The culture reinforced control, certainty, and fixed roles. It rewarded those who could make a plan and stick to it, regardless of whether that plan still made sense. I was taught to assume we could build a perfect roadmap: clear scope, set dates, defined budgets. But the reality was far messier. Business needs changed, technology evolved, people came and went. Agile asked us to embrace that mess, not resist it. It wasn't just about being flexible, it was about building a culture where uncertainty wasn't feared, but expected. Where collaboration mattered more than control, and were learning trumped perfection. That shift wasn't just professional, it was personal.

Honestly, I didn't expect much from the Agile training class, which was led by Angela Johnson, an upcoming Certified Scrum Trainer (CST) candidate. I figured it would be another dry, slide-heavy session, buzzwords, vague promises, and then back to the grind. But the trainer surprised me. She didn't just explain the mechanics of Agile, terms like sprints (short, focused work cycles), roles (defined team responsibilities), and backlogs (a prioritized list of work). She helped us see that Agile wasn't just a process, it was a fundamentally different way of working, one built on collaboration, adaptability, and continuous learning. She talked about trust. About psychological safety. About conversations that mattered. About giving teams the space to figure things out. As shown in **Figure 3.2**, I was thrilled to get my first certification.

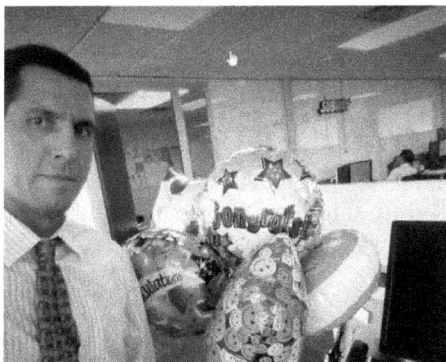

Figure 3.2: Receiving my first certification

It wasn't perfect, and I was still skeptical, but something in me started to shift. Not because I suddenly understood Agile, but because, for the first time, I felt like maybe there was another way to lead.

George made it clear: this wasn't about sticky notes and stand-ups, it was about culture. "Culture," he said, "is what people do when no one's watching." Transformation wasn't going to come from tools or meetings. It had to start with us, our mindset, our behavior, our values. That kind of change takes time. And courage. And it wasn't optional.

Then he did something bold, something that initially shocked me. He announced that everyone in technology would now report directly to him. My first thought was: 100 people reporting to one person? How will I ever get guidance? How will he monitor our performance? At the time, it felt unmanageable. Too much. Too fast. But looking back, I see the wisdom in it. By centralizing leadership, he removed unnecessary layers of management that often slowed things down. It gave us the clarity, focus, and freedom we needed to align, experiment, and evolve, without extra bureaucracy getting in the way.

That cultural shift didn't stay in our minds, it reshaped our environment.

Around the same time, George introduced IPC's revised core values: *Franchisee Focus, Humble Professional,* and *Make Things Happen.* I had worked for several companies before IPC, but honestly, I couldn't recall a single core value from any of them. These were different, simple, memorable, and lived out in the way we actually worked. They weren't just words on a wall.

They grounded us during uncertain times and made it easier to move forward without a long list of rules or micromanagement.

Over time I began to notice something deeper. The values were never meant to stand alone. Each one by itself could lean too far in one direction, but together they created balance. *Franchisee Focus* kept our attention on who we served, *Humble Professional* kept our egos in check, and *Make Things Happen* reminded us to take ownership and get things done. Together they became a compass we could rely on to guide decisions and behavior.

Not long after, I asked George what his vision for Agile was. He told me he wanted to build a world-class Agile organization. That conversation changed me. I didn't suddenly feel ready, but I felt challenged and excited to figure it out. From that point on, I didn't need step-by-step direction. The vision gave me purpose, and the values gave me clarity. I still bounced ideas around and asked for feedback, but I never felt pressured to do things someone else's way. For the first time in my career, leadership felt less like control and more like trust, alignment, and shared purpose.

Around the same time, George introduced IPC's revised core values: *Franchisee Focus, Humble Professional,* and *Make Things Happen.* I had worked for several companies before IPC, but honestly, I couldn't recall a single core value from any of them. These were different, simple, memorable, and lived out in the way we actually worked. They weren't just words on a wall. They grounded us during uncertain times and made it easier to move forward without a long list of rules or micromanagement.

Over time I began to notice something deeper. The values were never meant to stand alone. Each one by itself could lean too far in one direction, but together they created balance. *Franchisee*

Focus kept our attention on who we served, *Humble Professional* kept our egos in check, and *Make Things Happen* reminded us to take ownership and get things done. Together they became a compass we could rely on to guide decisions and behavior.

Not long after, I asked George what his vision for Agile was. He told me he wanted to build a world-class Agile organization. That conversation changed me. I didn't suddenly feel ready, but I felt challenged and excited to figure it out. From that point on, I didn't need step-by-step direction. The vision gave me purpose, and the values gave me clarity. I still bounced ideas around and asked for feedback, but I never felt pressured to do things someone else's way. For the first time in my career, leadership felt less like control and more like trust, alignment, and shared purpose.

And then came the physical changes.

Some leaders were asked to give up their private offices. Others volunteered. But they didn't just relocate, they let go of their titles. They gave up traditional management roles and embraced a new way of leading from within the team. Instead of corner offices, they sat shoulder to shoulder with their colleagues. Before the change, the office was filled with high cubicle walls that made collaboration difficult. As leaders moved out, those barriers came down. The spaces became open meeting rooms. At first, we just made do with what we had. The physical space took time to build out. We redesigned the office gradually to encourage interaction, writable whiteboard walls on every surface, fewer cubicle barriers, and an intentional layout that promoted collaboration. It was a message: we're not just changing how we work, we're changing how we show up for each other.

That message didn't just change how I worked, it redefined what kind of leader I wanted to become.

Key Learnings from Chapter 3

- True transformation starts with courageous leadership, not tools.
- Culture change begins with mindset, not mechanics.
- Agile is as much about values and behaviors as it is about practices and roles.
- Leading by example, especially through uncertainty, builds trust and momentum.

I thought we were changing how we worked. But what I didn't realize was that I was beginning to change too. What started as a company shift became a mirror, reflecting the kind of leader I was, and the kind I hoped to become. What I didn't know yet was that the hardest part of transformation wasn't learning new practices. It was letting go of old ones.

Everything was about to accelerate.

Chapter 4:

Building the Agile Team

W e stood at the edge of change, excited, unsure, and aware that there was no turning back. Agile wasn't just a new way of working, it was a new way of being. The ideas from our training sounded great, but now we had to put them into action. Our leaders wanted Agile teams, and we needed to figure out how to make that real. This was the beginning of many team building activities, as captured in **Figure 4.1**

Figure 4.1: What does it take to build a team?

I began to think about what really drives a team forward. It's not just roles or processes, it's momentum, clarity, and meaningful work. When that work is missing or delayed, progress stalls. Even the most talented team can't deliver if they're left waiting on decisions or facing constant changes in direction. Agile can accommodate shifting priorities when they are intentional and tied to delivering value, but if those shifts are driven by chasing a new shiny object every week, momentum breaks down. To thrive, teams need more than tasks, they need purpose and alignment.

We reorganized our technology department into smaller teams, around 7 to 9 members each. People who used to be Project Managers took on new roles as Product Owners and Scrum Masters. A **Product Owner** focuses on defining and prioritizing the most valuable work for the team, while a **Scrum Master** supports the team by facilitating communication, removing obstacles, and fostering continuous improvement.

To support broader collaboration, we brought in shared services, teams like Database, Infrastructure, and Security, early into planning ceremonies.

These teams were cross-functional, meaning people with different skills, developers, designers, testers, worked together from start to finish. Some had never worked this closely before. It wasn't always easy. Some were shy. Some didn't like change. I worried it wouldn't work.

> **Coaching Guidance:**
> If you haven't experienced working in a cross-functional team, think of it like planning a wedding: the Product Owner decides what's needed, the Scrum Master coordinates like a planner, and the team brings different skills, like caterers and musicians, all working together for one successful event.

As project managers, many of us felt lost. Our job titles changed, but we didn't know exactly what our new roles meant. It was hard to guide others when we didn't feel grounded ourselves.

But instead of pausing, we kept going. We experimented with structure, created rhythms to support coordination, and slowly began to align around purpose.

Laying the Groundwork

We didn't have all the answers, but we committed to starting. Our focus was simple: bring teams together to communicate better and grow together. By creating dedicated cross-functional teams, we gave people the opportunity to work side by side, build relationships, and develop shared ownership.

Before we could build high-performing teams, we had to understand the person we often overlook, ourselves.

The Journey Inward

But this wasn't immediate. In fact, it was turbulent.

Something unexpected and heartbreaking happened. My PMO manager, my mentor, the one who had started our book club and someone I deeply respected, was let go. She had always been a champion of learning and growth, and it hurt to see her leave. Her departure shook me. It reminded me that not everyone thrives in an Agile environment, or maybe we hadn't done enough to support her through the transition.

The shift didn't start with a breakthrough, it started with resistance, confusion, and discomfort. It reminded me of the classic J-curve of change, where performance or confidence dips before it improves. We hit that low point before we began to climb. People didn't transform right away. Many were skeptical. Some resisted. Some felt lost. And that was okay. Over time, moments of connection like the one captured in **Figure 4.2** showed us what building trust truly looked like.

Figure 4.2: This is what building trust really looks like!

As George once said, "True transformation isn't sparked by tools, it's rooted in mindset. Agile isn't about checklists. It's about how we think, how we behave, and how we collaborate. And at the center of it all is belief, what we value, what we reinforce, and how we choose to show up for one another. Culture is what people do when no one's watching. If people believe in transparency, they'll live it. If they value teamwork, they'll lean into it, even without being told."

Agile transformation challenged more than our process, it challenged our identity. I heard someone say once, "It's just a job, I'm not here to make friends." That perspective created a real challenge for me. It felt like a defense mechanism, a way to stay emotionally detached. In contrast, some leaders would often say, "Leave your ego at the door." That message landed differently. It felt like an invitation to grow, to listen, and to lead with humility. Both sayings came from different places and shaped how people showed up. But even good advice can be taken too far. Growth requires balance. It takes ongoing reflection and the courage to ask, "How am I coming across?"

I struggled with this. My instinct was to jump in and fix problems, to move fast and take control. But I began to realize that leadership wasn't about doing more or less. It was about working smarter, being intentional, and building solutions that would last. Real leadership meant slowing down just enough to really listen, understand the bigger picture, and help others grow with me. That mindset shift wasn't easy, but it reshaped how I showed up, not just at work, but with my family, my friends, and in every part of my life.

Still, I had to watch the line between reflection and self-criticism. I gave myself 24 hours. I'd review what went wrong, learn, and move on. Like a basketball player who misses a shot, reset, refocus, take another shot.

The journey toward self-awareness didn't end, it evolved. It continued to shape how we worked, led, and grew together.

This wasn't a textbook implementation. It was hands-on, imperfect, and grounded in our reality. But the connection between inner awareness and external alignment made it work. As I learned more about myself, I began to see how those insights applied not just to me, but to how we structured teams, planned work, and communicated across the organization.

While most teams settled into Scrum, my journey looked different. Letting go of structure and embracing uncertainty wasn't easy. But it helped me grow, not just in my role, but in how I led.

Key Learnings from Chapter 4

- High-performing teams don't emerge from structure alone. They are built through shared purpose, trust, and care.
- Resistance and confusion are part of every transformation. Growth begins when people feel safe enough to push through it.
- Losing champions during change is painful, but those moments reveal the importance of resilience and collective ownership.
- The best Agile structures are not copied from a framework. They are discovered through experimentation and adaptation.

We weren't just adopting Agile. We were building a culture, one rooted in care, alignment, and shared ownership. A culture we would continue to test, strengthen, and grow together.

Chapter 5:

Finding Flow with Kanban

Trust is fragile. It doesn't come with a title, and it can't be demanded. It's built slowly, through actions, consistency, and the moments you choose to stand with others.

While other teams were starting to find their groove with Scrum, my assignment was different. I was placed with the infrastructure team, a group whose work didn't fit neatly into Scrum's timeboxes or ceremonies. At first, I thought I could just apply the same approach everyone else was using. I was wrong. **Figure 5.1** showcases some of the members of the infrastructure team.

Figure 5.1: IPC's Infrastructure Team

That's when we stumbled across something called Kanban. Honestly, the name made me think of a martial art. For a second,

I imagined bowing into a dojo instead of walking into a meeting room. But this "strange new thing" turned out to be exactly what we needed.

Think of Kanban like a simple visual map for getting work done. The columns represent the big steps, gathering requirements, planning or designing the solution, building it, testing it, and finally deploying it. The rows can act like lanes for different types of work, one lane for small projects, another for large projects, and one for operations or support. The goal is straightforward: watch your work move steadily from left to right until it's done.

When I first saw Kanban, it looked too simple, just columns and sticky notes. But after reading David Anderson's book, it clicked. Kanban meets a team where they are, visualizes work, limits work in progress (WIP), and helps identify and remove obstacles. My new role as Kanban Master wasn't just about managing flow, it was about building trust, delivering faster, and nurturing the team's growth.

Our first physical board was plain: masking tape lines on a wall with stickies to track tasks, as shown in **Figure 5.2**. I learned early on never to make the lanes perfectly straight, because a rigid design makes it harder to adapt later. Just like in life, chasing perfection can keep you from evolving. Over time, the board grew more sophisticated: swim lanes/rows for priority work, WIP limits to prevent overload, and team photos to mark blockers, playful, visual nudges that spurred action without blame. Visibility made bottlenecks impossible to ignore, and because they were out in the open, fixing them became a shared responsibility.

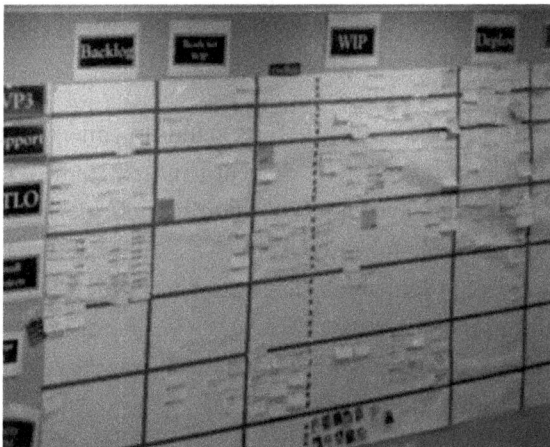

Figure 5.2: Clarity, Flow, Focus. That's the power of Kanban.

While development teams ran Scrum, we added additional lanes to align with them. Physical boards, no digital tools yet, turned our workspace into a live hub for collaboration. We also held daily stand-ups, short, focused meetings where each team member shared what they accomplished yesterday, what they were working on today, and any obstacles in their way. The goal was to maintain visibility, align quickly, and address issues early. But even with a well-designed board and regular stand-ups, I still felt like an outsider. The team saw me as a manager, not one of them.

That changed during a brutal 48-hour data center relocation. I could have stayed home and "managed," providing status updates and reports, but instead I was there, lifting servers, pulling cables, freezing in that meat-locker of a room. At first, it was awkward, what was I doing there? But gradually, the conversations began to include me. By the end of those long, cold hours, I wasn't fully one of them yet, but I was closer. No longer just a manager, I was beginning to feel like a teammate. The next chapter of our relationship came quickly, in a moment that truly broke the ice and solidified that bond.

One day during the infrastructure stand-up, one of our team members, Lito, asked if I'd heard about the new Agile methodology, "Jabbawockeez." I didn't catch the joke at first. Later, I found out Jabbawockeez was a dance crew, not a framework. See a Jabbawockeez poster in **Figure 5.3**. But they kept it going, day after day. "Rick, are we going to implement Jabbawockeez next week?" "Did the CIO approve it?" I had enough. I decided to flip the script.

Figure 5.3: The Agile-wockeez.

I got approval from Tony, our infrastructure director, to prank them back. The next morning in our stand-up, I came in dead serious. "Guys," I said, "I talked to George, our CIO. He's really excited about this Jabbawockeez approach that you discovered. He'd like the team to present it to him next week." Their faces froze. One of them dropped his coffee. Another muttered. After the stand-up, they pulled me aside to confess it was a prank. I responded, "You've got to be kidding me."

I stood up, looking frustrated, and walked out of the room. They ran straight to Tony, worried they'd crossed a line. He told them that I was really upset. The prank worked so well because I sold it, walking out in frustration made it believable, and all the more hilarious when they realized they'd been had.

An hour later, I let them off the hook. I laughed harder than anyone, gotcha! They enjoyed seeing that I could take a joke, and dish it out just as well. That moment sealed us. We weren't just a team, we were a tribe. The same playful spirit that bonded us through that prank also fueled a deeper pride in who we were and what we could contribute.

As our bond strengthened, the infrastructure team wanted to share their work and identity with others. Infrastructure, Security, and Support are often underappreciated, so we began a tradition of after-work gatherings that highlighted our people as much as our projects.

Team Showcase

These weren't status updates. They were informal gatherings with food, music, and laughter, where teams showed off their uniqueness and their culture. Some drew from our Latin roots, with card games and dominoes that made the office feel like family. These simple traditions broke down walls and built connections across teams, reminding us we were more than our roles.

Just like the prank showed our humor, these showcases highlighted our pride. Both moments proved that trust grows not only from the work itself, but from the way we connected and celebrated as people. Below in **Figure 5.4**, there is a picture of the team bonding during lunch.

Figure 5.4: One table, one team, IPC lunch style.

The showcases became another way of strengthening trust. They reminded us that our culture wasn't only about solving technical problems, it was also about celebrating who we were together. That sense of pride and connection carried over into our daily work. As months passed, our Kanban board evolved like a living organism, adapting as we learned. Bottlenecks weren't blame points; they were challenges we tackled together.

The work flowed, the team grew stronger, and in August 2012, Gartner recognized our implementation, even featuring a photo of our original board, tape, stickies, imperfect lanes, and all. The validation was great, but the real prize was the team we had built.

Kanban gave us flow. Trust made it unstoppable.

Key Learnings from Chapter 5

- Frameworks work best when adapted to the team, not the other way around.
- Trust grows when leaders join the struggle, not just manage it.
- Shared traditions and humor build belonging as much as process improvements do.
- Flow is not just about efficiency; it is about momentum and pride in shared progress.

When you build trust, create visibility, and let the team own the flow, you're not just improving a process, you're transforming how people work together, and that's where the real magic happens.

Chapter 6:

From Kanban Master to Scrum Master

Before I could lead, I had to earn their trust. By mid-2013, I transitioned from Kanban Master to Scrum Master for the VP3 Team at IPC, titles didn't mean much, what mattered was how you showed up, how you contributed, and whether the team trusted you enough to let you in.

An open Scrum Master position became available when Bob, the previous Scrum Master, had transitioned into the team to focus on quality assurance.

Bob is one of a kind. At first, he can come across as intense, aggressive, and direct. But once you get to know him, you realize he's driven by a deep sense of purpose and an unwavering commitment to doing what's best for the company. A man of faith, Bob had a favorite saying. Anytime someone asked, "How are you doing today, Bob?" he'd respond with a smile, "Too blessed to be stressed." Later we created a shirt to capture motto, **Figure 6.1** shows Bob wearing his shirt.

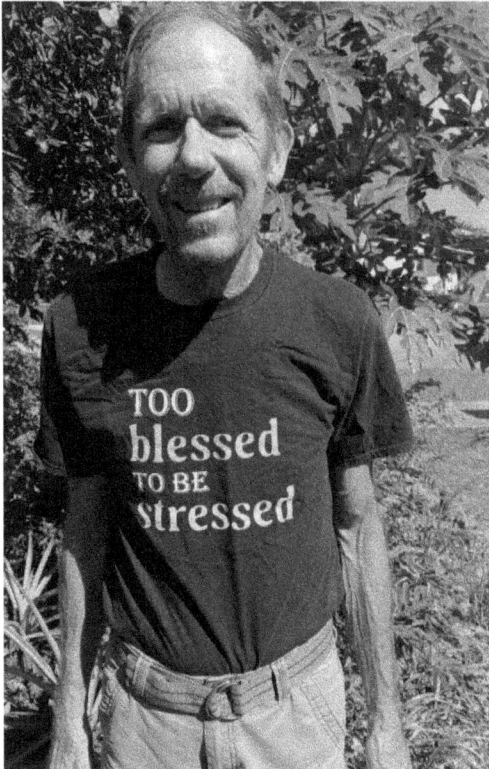

Figure 6.1: Too Blessed to be Stressed

Before I could join the team, they interviewed me directly, no leadership panel, just developers, QA, operations, and the Product Owner. They asked tough questions about how I handled conflict, whether I'd overridden team decisions, and how I viewed the Scrum Master role. They wanted to ensure I wasn't another manager in disguise, but someone who would listen, protect their space, and add value. This wasn't just any team. They owned the company's most critical application: the credit card processing system serving over 30,000 Subway stores. High visibility, high stakes, zero room for ego. If the system went down for just a few minutes, it could cost millions. The team voted, and I was approved. I accepted the challenge with humility, knowing I had to prove myself again.

The Offsite

After a few months, we brought the team together for an offsite at Dave & Buster's. Most of the developers were already in Miami. We started the day in a conference room, where I facilitated a team values exercise. While company values set the tone, the heartbeat of a great team comes from the culture they create for themselves. Our values became commitment, integrity, communication, respect, fun, and excellence, better known as "awesomeness."

From there, we moved into strategy, vision, and roadmap sessions, as shown in **Figure 6.2**. Asking thoughtful questions at this stage made a world of difference. The conversations were direct, client-focused, spirited, and grounded in accountability.

Figure 6.2: VP3 Team in Action

We finished the day with a retrospective, where Jason, one of our talented developers, made his mark. A remote teammate whose workspace resembled a command center of glowing screens, he was deeply immersed in the technical side of his craft: focused, precise, relentless. At the time, he seemed more comfortable with systems than with people, and I assumed that explained his reluctance during these sessions. That impression, however, turned out to be only part of the story.

During that discussion, Jason challenged their efficiency, questioning whether they truly lived up to the values we had just defined. For him, retrospectives often felt like they produced little return on investment. He wanted issues surfaced quickly, not every two weeks simply because Scrum prescribed it. Over time, I came to understand his critique not as resistance, but as a valuable push for us to make retrospectives more effective.

To break through some of the tension, I decided to use humor. I told Jason, "If I can write your network password on this piece of paper, you have to give retrospectives an honest shot." He looked puzzled, almost calculating the odds. "You must've talked to infrastructure," he guessed. "Nope," I replied. When he finally agreed, I flipped the paper over, it read, "your network password." He smirked, and that crack in his seriousness opened the door to making retrospectives feel less rigid and more creative. Sometimes we dropped templates and just talked. Other times we focused on data. I even rotated facilitation to encourage shared ownership. Gradually, the team, including Jason, began to see retrospectives as more valuable when they were flexible and real.

We wrapped up the retro around 5 p.m., and the mood was lighter than when we started. Since the offsite was held in a separate conference room at Dave & Buster's, we moved directly from work to fun. The arcade was buzzing with neon lights, clinking tokens, and bursts of laughter, and **Figure 6.3** shows how we were enjoying this experience. Bob was hunched over a Skee-Ball

Lane, Jason locked in on a shooter game, and other teammates spread out across air hockey, racing games, and basketball hoops. I found myself laughing harder than I had in months. For a night, we weren't just developers, testers, and coaches, we were people, playing, connecting, belonging.

Figure 6.3: From retro to arcade fun—work ended, laughter began

Psychological Safety in Action

One of the most powerful demonstrations of this culture came several months later during a retrospective when our CIO, George, accidentally walked in. Bob stood up and calmly asked him to leave, reminding him it was team space. George thanked him and left. That simple act reinforced psychological safety.

Agile Is Earned

In my training classes today, I emphasize: Agile isn't given, it's earned. I often joke by singing, "You have to fight for your right... to be Agile!" It always gets a laugh, and it sticks in people's minds. Humor aside, the message is serious. Agile is earned when teams:

- Live their values
- Own commitments
- Have difficult conversations
- Embrace transparency
- Commit to continuous improvement

Without this commitment, empowerment won't last.

Engineering Excellence

The team kept raising the bar. They automated testing early, built security into development, and ensured fast feedback loops. A real-time dashboard flashed red the moment someone broke the build, sparking immediate accountability. **Figure 6.4** shows the real time dashboard. As Ariel, our influential tech lead, often said: "If your pipeline to delivery is painful, do it more, not less. Repetition forces efficiency."

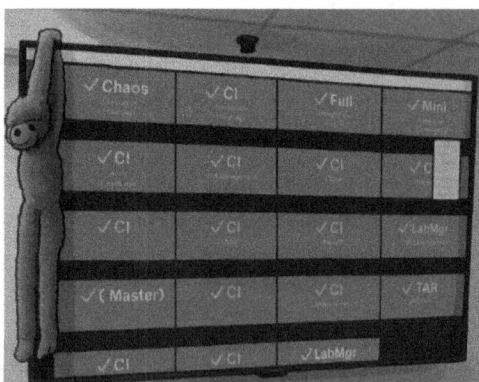

Figure 6.4: All Green, All Good

Continuing to Mature

The VP3 team matured into one of the highest-performing groups I've ever worked with:

- Delivering weekly to a mission-critical system without major issues
- Interviewing and selecting their own teammates
- Evaluating performance as a team, not individuals

Ariel modeled true leadership, not by authority but by empowerment. He proved there's a world of difference between a manager saying, "you're behind" and a teammate saying, "we need you."

The VP3 team's success came from trust, accountability, and shared purpose. Leadership created the right environment, and the team proved they deserved it. And they never stopped evolving.

Key Learnings from Chapter 6

- Trust is earned, not given. Teams choose who they let in as a leader.
- Psychological safety must be protected, even when executives are in the room.
- Shared experiences inside and outside of work strengthen bonds and fuel performance.
- Continuous improvement has the greatest impact when it is owned and shaped by the team itself.

Becoming a Scrum Master wasn't about leading the team, it was about learning from them. I didn't earn their trust with titles or tools, I earned it by showing up, listening, and caring. What transformed us wasn't process, it was people. And in the end, that team didn't just teach me how to coach, they taught me how to lead.

Chapter 7:

From Internal Growth to Community Impact

It started with ten people, a few pizzas, and a shared hunger for something better. The momentum we built at IPC didn't stay within our walls. As our Agile maturity deepened, so did a shared desire to connect outward, to give back, to learn, and to build something bigger than ourselves.

It started small. I launched an Agile meetup with a few colleagues who had attended an Agile Palooza event. We called it the South Florida Agile Association, SFAA for short. **Figure 7.1** shows first steps of the SFAA,

Figure 7.1: Coaches learning, growing, and having a blast together

The first gathering? Just ten people. A few slices of pizza. A few folding chairs. But the conversations were rich, and the energy was undeniable. The simplicity made it special, we weren't just meeting, we were building a movement.

We met monthly in different locations throughout Dade and Broward County, swapping stories and strategies. Titles didn't matter, Scrum Masters, developers, coaches, or simply Agile-curious, everyone had a voice. The community grew steadily. Ten became twenty. Then fifty. Then hundreds. I am grateful for the amazing people I met during this journey. Marcelo Lopez (Yoda, walking encyclopedia) from day one did not miss a meeting and was always providing a helping hand. The best part of the journey was building a lasting relationship with him, as shown in **Figure 7.2**.

Figure 7.2: Rick and Marcelo

As a Scrum Master, and someone leading the transformation, you don't always get to bounce ideas around. Many of the challenges involve personal dynamics, which can feel isolating. These meetups gave me a great way to connect, share, experiment, and learn from others. It was like finding a group that spoke the same language.

One of my favorite memories was hosting a meetup right at IPC. We brought in two massive six-foot Subway sandwiches and gathered in the large conference room. **Figure 7.3** shows that I'm not lying about the size of the sandwich. The place filled quickly, not just with the smell of fresh bread, but with curiosity and excitement. James Grenning, one of the original authors of the Agile Manifesto, joined us to speak about Test-Driven Development (TDD). TDD is like writing a to-do list before you clean your house. You make a list of what "done" looks like, then check off each task as you go. If something's missing, the list helps you spot it fast.

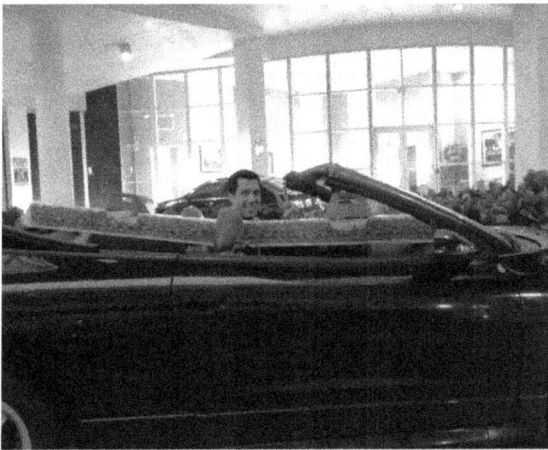

Figure 7.3: When Agile meets a six-foot sandwich.

James volunteered his time, like so many of our amazing speakers over the years. He was incredibly humble, not what I expected from someone who had achieved so much success. You might think that someone so influential would carry themselves with a certain ego, but James showed the opposite. His approach mirrored the very essence of Agile, empowering others, creating space, and letting the team shine.

One thing James said that really stuck with me was: "Talk to each other, people. At the end of the day, problems will be solved when people come together to have the uncomfortable conversations and do what's best for the company." That insight resonated with all of us navigating complex environments, reminding us that the toughest problems often require courage, connection, and candid conversations.

That night, it became clear: Agile wasn't just a set of practices, it was a living community, and we were part of its heartbeat. The momentum of these meetups naturally evolved into something bigger.

High Performing Teams Conference (HPTC)

The success of our meetups sparked a bigger idea: What if we took this energy and scaled it into a full conference?

As we expanded, we moved to running Agile conferences for a larger audience. Our first Agile conference was free to the public. It was hosted at IPC in October 2013 and reached a maximum capacity of 200 attendees: the High Performing Teams Conference (HPTC).

This was a great day, we were ready. I had a plethora of IPC team members prepared to make the experience unforgettable, from Bob directing people to their parking spaces to HR welcoming them with a smile at the registration desk, as shown in **Figure 7.4**. Slowly, the attendees entered the room, not knowing what a special experience was about to unfold.

Figure 7.4: Guided in with care, greeted with a smile.

That morning, I felt insecure about how many people would actually show up, and I was nervous about whether they would enjoy the session. It was my first big conference that I was responsible for, and the pressure weighed on me. As the morning keynote, I simply shared stories from the front lines—how we built high-performing teams at IPC and what made them work. It wasn't theory, it was lived experience. We talked about the traits that kept showing up: trust, ownership, shared values, continuous improvement, and a genuine sense of fun and passion. **Figure 7.5** shows the opening keynote.

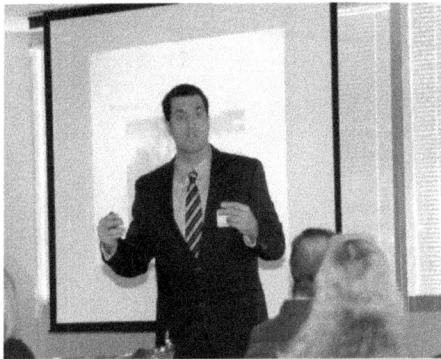

Figure 7.5: Rick's opening at HPTC

At first, I worried my nerves would show, but as I shared those real stories, the energy in the room shifted. People leaned in, connected, and I realized that authenticity mattered far more than perfection.

After my keynote, we reconfigured the rooms for breakout sessions where additional speakers could present. Several of the speakers were from IPC like Ariel. They did an amazing job, and the feedback we received was overwhelmingly positive. Lunch, of course, featured Subway subs, and just when I thought the day couldn't get any better, HR surprised everyone with ice cream at 2 p.m.

Our CEO, Jan Risi, delivered the closing keynote. **Figure 7.6** showcases her presentation. It was the first time I'd heard her speak publicly about Agile, and I was eager to hear her perspective. Jan closed the conference with a surprising analogy, comparing Agile to training her dog. At first, it caught me off guard, but her message was clear: Agile isn't about control, it's about trust, patience, and building the kind of relationship where people feel safe to grow.

Figure 7.6: Jan's closing keynote.

That moment, hearing our CEO close the day by publicly aligning with Agile, brought it all together. It showed how far the movement had grown within IPC and validated the culture we had built from the ground up

The conference became an annual tradition, growing year after year, eventually drawing over 600 participants. As our reach expanded beyond Florida, we rebranded the event to the Agile International Conference (AIC) to reflect our global impact.

The response was overwhelming. We heard stories from people who had found jobs, leveled up their careers, and discovered a sense of belonging through the community. People told us it was the first time they felt truly seen in their Agile journey. For many, the conference wasn't just a professional event, it was a support system, a spark of inspiration, and a place to call home. It created momentum, connection, and belief that real change was not only possible but already happening all around us.

SFAA wasn't just about sharing Agile, it was about helping people free themselves from a lack of empowerment. It reminded us that transformation goes beyond tools and practices, it's about people discovering their voice, realizing their potential, and finding the courage to lead change. It wasn't just IPC's story anymore, it was becoming everyone's story.

To carry this spirit of community even further, I began looking for other professional circles where Agile thinking could make a difference. One of the most influential was the Project Management Institute (PMI), an organization close to my own roots.

Helping the South Florida PMI (Project Management Institute)

My journey with PMI was a natural extension of the community spirit we had built. I had been a member of the South Florida (PMI) chapter since earning my PMP early in my career, and I knew how influential the institute was for project leaders shaping the way organizations delivered value. I wanted to bring the same energy, openness, and agile mindset that had transformed IPC and the South Florida Agile Association into this professional circle.

I began volunteering with the South Florida PMI chapter, where I served for several years as the VP of Membership. Later, I was invited to coach the South Florida PMI board itself. My role was to help them mature as a leadership team and build muscle memory for an agile mindset. We experimented with running their major yearly events using agile practices, planning in iterations, adapting to change, and focusing on collaboration. One vivid memory was a big-room planning session for the upcoming yearly Project Management Conference (PMC). A few weeks prior I coached a small team to help with the facilitation.

That morning, we all came dressed in red shirts, as shown in **Figure 7.7**. We used Kanban boards to organize every detail of the event. Each task, from catering to speaker preparation, was visible, and board members could track progress as items moved across the board. For many, it was the first time project planning felt dynamic and collaborative rather than rigid and stressful. The success of that event showed them firsthand that agility wasn't just for software teams, it was a way to lead any organization with adaptability and trust.

Figure 7.7: From IPC to PMI, the journey continues

Key Learnings from Chapter 7

- Lasting movements often begin with small, simple gatherings.
- Community thrives when every voice is welcomed and valued.
- Sharing experiences beyond one organization amplifies transformation.
- Real discovery happens when leaders stop working in isolation and begin building with others.

We thought we were building a meetup. What we built was a movement. The heart of Agile wasn't just in our sprints or ceremonies, it was in the community that grew when we opened our doors and shared our stories. As we scaled beyond our walls, we realized the greatest impact wasn't what we accomplished alone, but what we inspired together. And that's how transformation became something much bigger than us. It also set the stage for what came next, when we decided to open our doors and invite the world inside to see our journey firsthand.

Chapter 8:

Opening Our Doors to the World

W hen we opened our doors, we did more than share Agile, we sparked belief. Just when it felt like we'd done it all, we launched something even more impactful.

Another powerful example of our commitment to community was the IPC Executive Agile Experience, an on-site event where we shared our Agile transformation through the voices of those directly involved. Presenters shared diverse perspectives, from the CIO to Product Owners, Scrum Masters, Infrastructure, Developers, Quality Assurance (QA), and Business teams, giving a full view of our journey and the lessons we learned together.

We started the IPC Executive Agile Experience by inviting our vendors. These were companies we worked with regularly, and we thought it was important to give them a clearer understanding of how we operated and where we were headed. As part of the experience, visitors were given a walk-through of our facility where they could observe stand-up meetings and witness real-time team interactions. After the initial walk-through, we brought the visitors into a meeting room designed for interaction, with whiteboards covering the walls to encourage collaboration and idea sharing. **Figure 8.1** showcases the participation in the icebreaker activity. I asked a simple question with a creative twist: what is your biggest challenge in delivering value to your customers? "Can you draw it?"

Figure 8.1: drawing challenges that fuel transformation.

The room filled with laughter and curiosity as people sketched out their daily frustrations. Guessing the meanings behind the drawings added a layer of fun and sparked authentic conversations. More importantly, it gave us real insight into their struggles, allowing us to adapt our presentations on the fly and make the experience even more relevant.

Following my kickoff activity, I passed the mic to George. As the executive sponsor who initiated the Agile transformation, he spoke with humility about the risks, lessons, and sleepless nights that came with leading change. What struck people most was not just his candor but his conviction. George often found it troubling that so many CIOs focused mainly on technology, when the real work of transformation was about culture, trust, and creating the environment for teams to succeed. That perspective resonated deeply with the room. For the executives in attendance, his story was more than a leadership account, it was a mirror reflecting what was possible in their own organizations. **Figure 8.2** illustrates participants attending the event.

Figure 8.2: Agile in action with CH Robinson.

After George, other presenters stepped forward to share their unique perspectives.

Product Owners Sion and Kelly-Ann highlighted the art of prioritization, describing how they balanced competing stakeholder demands while keeping customer value at the center. They explained how clearer priorities allowed teams to focus on what mattered most, reducing waste and increasing impact. Their stories illustrated how disciplined backlog management built trust and confidence with the business.

Scrum Master Christina and I spoke passionately about building psychological safety. Together we encouraged open dialogue, created space for differing opinions, and helped teams feel safe enough to take risks. By keeping teams focused on outcomes rather than rigid processes, we showed how Agile enabled stronger collaboration and resilience during times of uncertainty.

Developers Ariel and Daniel, along with QA member Bob, described the technical side of transformation. They spoke about breaking down silos between development and testing, adopting test automation, and continuously integrating code to catch issues early. Ariel often emphasized just how remarkable the shift had been, saying the development team had become nearly ten times more productive since adopting Agile. For him, "ten times" wasn't an exaggeration, it reflected a dramatic leap forward: faster time to market, consistently higher quality, quicker response times, and project releases so uneventful they became the norm rather than the exception. He also pointed to stronger business alignment and happier employees as powerful proof of transformation.

Infrastructure leader Fernando explained how his team shifted from being seen as a bottleneck to becoming a trusted partner. By embracing transparency and agility, they provided faster, more reliable support that enabled innovation. Business representatives added their perspective, sharing how the stronger partnership with IT allowed them to respond to market changes more quickly and confidently.

Together, these voices painted a vivid picture of transformation, showing Agile alive in many parts of the organization, even if it had not yet fully reached every role and function.

It's amazing how these presentations evolved. You could return in just a quarter and see a completely different presentation. We were constantly pushing ourselves to improve, always experimenting with new ideas, concepts, techniques, and tools. Failure was part of the process, and we embraced the ability to fail fast and learn quickly.

Held quarterly for several years, the event became so popular that it was often booked a year in advance. To our knowledge, no other organization was offering this kind of immersive, multi-role experience. We hosted over 80 companies, and even some of

Gartner's executive coaches began recommending the experience to their clients. **Figure 8.3** illustrates how, later in our journey, several of our board members even attended.

Figure 8.3: Board leaders joining the culture of openness.

The response was incredible. People didn't just appreciate the transparency, they left inspired. Watching their eyes light up and hearing their questions reminded me of the deeper purpose behind opening our doors. These weren't just visitors, they were future changemakers, and we had the chance to ignite something real. Over the years, I've met employees from various companies who proudly share their companies' Agile journeys, often unaware that their transformation was sparked by their executives attending our event.

The event was always free, a reflection of our commitment to giving without expecting anything in return. Many people have asked us what motivates us. Our answer is simple: by teaching, we learn to master. We take pride in knowing our value, and we believe in giving back. It's part of our culture, one rooted in generosity, learning, and purpose.

It positioned IPC as the clear leader in South Florida for spreading Agile knowledge and building a stronger, more connected Agile community. Recognition followed: the CIO 100 Award, InformationWeek's Top 500 Technology Innovators (2013), Computerworld's Best Places to Work (ranked #16 in 2014), the QSR Applied Technology Award, and the Hospitality Technology Edge Award. Take a look at them in **Figure 8.4**. These weren't just acknowledgments of innovation; they were tributes to the culture we had built.

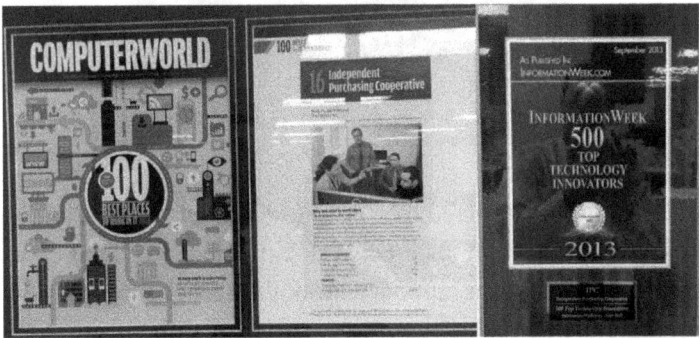

Figure 8.4: Recognitions

What began as a simple vendor visit turned into something much greater, a ripple effect that extended far beyond our office walls. By sharing our transformation openly, we didn't just showcase Agile practices, we sparked hope, connection, and possibility. We reminded people, ourselves included, that work can have meaning, and that culture, when nurtured, can become contagious.

Opening our doors wasn't the end of our journey. It was a new beginning, one that called us to look beyond what we had built and ask: How can we help others experience this too? That question would carry us even further.

Key Learnings from Chapter 8

- Transparency and authenticity spark belief and inspire change.
- Transformation resonates most when shared through real voices and lived experiences.
- Teaching openly is one of the best ways to deepen mastery.
- Culture becomes contagious when people witness what's truly possible.

We didn't open our doors to impress; we opened them to connect. What started as a simple tour became a spark for transformation across dozens of organizations. By sharing our story, we gave others permission to reimagine theirs. And in doing so, we discovered that the real power of Agile isn't just in how we work, it's in how we inspire change, one conversation at a time.

Chapter 9:

Culture of Care

The heart of Agile is simple: showing up for each other. I didn't learn that in training, it came in the quiet, unexpected moments when someone said, "I've got you."

Some of the most meaningful parts of our journey weren't tied to metrics or recognition. They were genuine acts of compassion that changed lives and shaped our culture forever.

At IPC, we created activities that brought us closer together: Bootcamps, Yoga sessions, 5k runs, Tough Mudder, and MS Bike Rides. **Figure 9.1** captures those adventures with dear coworkers and my son. These were energizing and reminded us we were more than colleagues. But beyond the camaraderie, three traditions stood out as defining expressions of who we were.

Figure 9.1: At IPC, bike rides and runs built bonds beyond work.

Community Volunteering

At IPC there were many opportunities to volunteer in the community. One program that stood out for me was KAPOW (Kids and the Power of Work), a national network of business-elementary school partnerships that introduces young students to work-related concepts and experiences that can be reinforced throughout their formative years.

I volunteered with my colleague Cindy for a specific class. The first day we visited the school brought back so many memories. Looking at the hallway, the tables, and the seats, I couldn't fathom being so small and fitting in those chairs. I have spoken at many events, but for some reason this was different. I was nervous, wondering if we would be able to get the kids excited about what we do and some of the lessons we hoped to share. Our topic was the importance of planning. My technique is always to get people moving to break the ice. Wow, was that a mistake. Kids have a certain pitch when they are all screaming at the same time that vibrates in your heart. Luckily, their teacher stayed in the room and knew what to do to calm them down. We came to teach, and here we were learning right from the start. Once calm was restored, we continued our activity by showing them the importance of a checklist, how it can help you see progress and not forget important details.

Looking back, I think we did okay. The kids were very attentive, which was a win in itself. We continued every two weeks and were so sad when the program ended. I'm happy to share my certificate of participation in **Figure 9.2**.

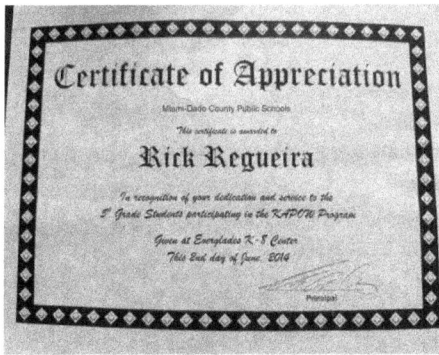

Figure 9.2: A moment of love, a memory for life.

At IPC I worked with Cindy as a Product Owner for the Database team. Today, I can't remember a single project we completed together, but I can definitely remember our contribution to the KAPOW program. The kids' smiling faces are engraved in our hearts.

While serving the community showed us the joy of giving outward, we also discovered powerful ways of caring inward, supporting each other in life's hardest moments.

Love Attack

One of our most heartfelt traditions was the "Love Attack." These spontaneous rallies brought teams together to support coworkers in need, cleaning homes, painting rooms, running errands, or simply showing up. It wasn't in anyone's job description, but it quickly became part of our identity. See some of the activities in **Figure 9.3**. These moments revealed that real teamwork extends far beyond the office walls.

Figure 9.3: Love Attack in Action

Shaved Heads

There I was preparing myself for a town hall meeting. Little did I know that I would lose something that day. After the meeting, a whisper moved through the audience that an employee had been diagnosed with cancer and would soon begin chemotherapy. This person was always amazing to work with, giving, supportive, and full of kindness. The news brought back memories of close friends and family members I had known whose lives were cut short by cancer.

Somehow, we were asked if we wanted to participate in shaving our hair as a sign of solidarity. I had never shaved my head before, but I did not hesitate for a minute. Seeing how many people participated, and how naturally everyone stepped forward, was inspiring. The unity and compassion in that moment were overwhelming. It was a visible, powerful way to say, "We're with you." See team photo in **Figure 9.4**.

Figure 9.4: United in compassion

That day, I felt the true power of culture, how simple acts of empathy could bring us together in ways no policy ever could. It showed us that it was okay to simply be ourselves and stand with one another, even in the hardest moments.

Personal Loss and Belonging

While these traditions showed our unity at work, nothing prepared me for how deeply I would feel it in my own life.

Life brings you amazing times, but also difficult ones. During my years at IPC, we shared both joy and hardship. We walked alongside colleagues as they faced personal struggles, and we mourned together when loved ones left us too soon.

For me, the hardest moment was losing my dear mother. She was the most caring and loving person I have ever known, the kind of person who would give her last dollar to make sure her family was okay. Losing her left a space nothing else could fill. See in **Figure 9.5** my mom and I. Te amo Mima.

Figure 9.5: A moment of love, a memory for life.

At the church for my mother's special service, my IPC family showed up. Their presence caught me by surprise. You make friends at work, but you don't always realize how deep those bonds run until life tests you. That day, I understood the true meaning of belonging. I am eternally grateful for the way my colleagues stood by me when I needed it most.

These experiences reminded us that compassion wasn't an initiative, it was who we were. This kind of compassion built unshakable trust, and trust built unstoppable teams. In those moments of kindness, we didn't just build connection, we built the backbone of our culture, the secret to our strength.

Agile gave us structure, but compassion gave it meaning. Without trust, collaboration, and empathy, no framework can succeed.

Key Learnings from Chapter 9

- Culture is proven in how people show up for each other in hard times, not in slogans or posters.
- Simple traditions and acts of compassion create bonds that no policy can replicate.
- Belonging is built when empathy becomes part of daily behavior.
- Discovery deepens when we realize leadership is as much about care as it is about results.

Those moments taught me that culture isn't built in meetings, but in how we choose to show up for one another. Agile gave us the tools, but compassion gave us soul. In the end, it wasn't the ceremonies or frameworks that defined us, but the compassion that carried us through. That was our true culture of care.

Chapter 10:

Coaching the Coaches

W hen to Hold On, When to Let Go. "A coach is not the one who provides the answers, but the one who helps you discover your own."

When I stepped into the role of Agile Coach, I quickly realized that coaching wasn't about having all the answers. It was about unlocking what was already within others. It meant listening deeply, observing carefully, and creating the conditions for people to find their own voice. That shift changed not just how I worked, but how I lived. By this stage in my journey, I had grown beyond the role of Scrum Master and stepped fully into the position of Agile Coach. I was no longer focused on just one team. I was now supporting multiple Agile teams, leading the Scrum Master Chapter, and guiding organizational change. The responsibility was greater, but so was the opportunity: to help teams thrive and to mentor other coaches as they expanded their influence.

See in **Figure 10.1** some of the best coaches I've ever had the privilege to meet.

Figure 10.1: Feel the vibe of the coaches

Some say you should never take work personally. I believe the opposite. Being a Scrum Master or Agile Coach means stepping into people's shoes, feeling their frustration, their doubt, and their hopes. Many nights I came home still carrying the weight of someone else's struggle. I remember one Scrum Master confiding that they felt like a failure because their team was constantly fighting. I carried that weight home, replaying the conversation in my mind, and worked with them to find small wins that rebuilt trust. Those experiences were heavy, but they were also a gift. They reminded me that sensitivity is not weakness, it is what makes the best Agile Coaches stand out. It is not a switch you turn on or off, it is part of who you are. That ability to feel deeply doesn't just shape your work, it shapes your life.

I was fortunate to have incredible people around me who made that transition easier. **Figure 10.2** shows the IPC coaches bonding together over lunch.

Figure 10.2: Where ideas flow as smoothly as the coffee.

Christina Alonso, my peer and fellow Agile Coach, was one of those people. She challenged me when it mattered most. Christina had a playful style, sometimes snapping a photo of my expression in a meeting and later teasing, "What were you thinking here?" Her humor created space for deeper conversations. What made our relationship powerful was how we balanced each other. She was the realist, thoughtful and thorough. I was the risk taker, energetic and quick to see challenges as opportunities. She grounded me when I was moving too fast, and I encouraged her when caution held her back. That partnership showed me that true growth happens when differences are met with trust, not division.

But not every coaching relationship worked out that way. Within our team of coaches, there was one colleague we simply couldn't connect with, no matter how much effort we put in. From the beginning, our conversations with her felt combative, as if she needed to prove she was the smartest in the room. Truthfully, she may have been. But her confrontational style made collaboration nearly impossible. We tried resets, group coaching, and fresh starts more than once, yet nothing shifted. Over time, we realized that not every connection can be forced, and our focus was better placed on the relationships where trust and growth could actually take root. She eventually moved on to a different job, and we still wished her well. That experience taught me that letting go is sometimes an act of wisdom, not defeat.

These contrasting experiences, one of balance and growth, the other of friction and release, shaped how I showed up in larger efforts like the IT restructuring. From Christina, I learned the value of curiosity and balance. From the difficult coach, I learned that not every battle is worth fighting. Both lessons reminded me that empowerment works best when grounded in respect, humility, and a clear understanding of where to invest energy.

Restructuring Through Empowerment

The restructuring of the IT department was not just an organizational exercise. It was a chance to apply everything I had learned about coaching: balancing perspectives, letting go when needed, and creating the conditions for people to step into their own power.

At the end of a quarterly town hall, I introduced an activity designed to give everyone a voice in shaping our future. I outlined the challenges we faced so people understood the why behind the change. The response was powerful. People openly acknowledged the issues, and you could feel the collective agreement that restructuring was needed. That sense of shared recognition gave everyone ownership.

We then elected representatives from each area, ensuring voices from every level of IT. These representatives formed a working group where healthy debates and shared decision-making became the norm. I'll never forget one developer who said after a session,

"This is the first time I feel like I had a say in how we're structured." That reaction proved empowerment was real.

Together, we built an initial backlog and worked in an Agile way to co-create the new structure. Transparency was key. This group provided open demos to the IT department to show progress and gather feedback. It was humbling to witness.

As coaches, we reviewed the makeup of the new teams. First, we looked for the cross-functional skill sets needed for success. The fewer dependencies a team has, the more it can own its solution. But skills alone can only take you so far. Next came culture, compatibility, and diversity, factors that give a team its true advantage. Finally, we drew from what we had learned through Belbin, the Five Dysfunctions, and Tribal Leadership.

> **Coaching Guidance:**
>
> If you want to strengthen your coaching impact, a few resources stand out. *Tribal Leadership* highlights the power of culture in shaping performance. *The Five Dysfunctions of a Team* uncovers common barriers to trust and collaboration. Belbin's Team Roles helps leaders understand how diverse strengths create balance. Together, these tools provide a practical foundation for building high-performing teams.

I often leaned on Belbin's Team Roles during team formation workshops, helping people recognize not just their technical skills but the unique strengths they brought to the group. Those conversations shifted the way teams saw themselves and each other, building trust that carried into their work.

I also drew on Tribal Leadership when coaching leadership teams, using its framework to help them recognize the cultural stage they were operating in and what it would take to move to the next level. And when teams hit conflict or mistrust, The Five Dysfunctions of a Team became a roadmap for addressing the root causes, guiding conversations about accountability, trust, and results.

The result? Teams were more aligned, morale improved, and delivery cycles shortened proof that empowerment wasn't just a philosophy, it was a strategy.

I started as someone who measured success in dates and deadlines. Now, I saw success in connection, clarity, and courage. I wasn't just helping teams do Agile, I was helping them be Agile. And in doing so, I became a better version of myself.

Key Learnings from Chapter 10

- Coaching creates the space for growth; it's not about having all the answers.
- Trust and balance in partnerships strengthen leadership and resilience.
- Knowing when to hold on and when to let go is essential for empowering others.

Coaching didn't just shape the leader I became. It reshaped the person I was becoming. That is where the heart of leadership lives, and that is what makes this work unforgettable.

Chapter 11:

Bridging the Gap: Coaching Across the Enterprise

B ridging IT and the business was never just about process, it was about breaking through fear. Fear of the unknown. Fear of change. Fear of losing control. The real challenge wasn't in teaching practices, it was in creating courage across an organization that had lived in silos for years. In many ways, this chapter begins and ends with the same truth: courage and connection will always outlast control.

That's when I stepped into a broader role: moving from Agile Coach to Enterprise Coach. For me, the title was never the focus, it was about expanding my influence. Each role didn't mean more importance, just different responsibilities. As the teams and organization matured, so did I. My growth was directly tied to theirs.

One of the biggest lessons I learned was the importance of giving people space, especially high-performing teams. Many of the same tools I used at the team level applied just as effectively across programs and portfolios. But the key was always this: meet people where they are. See in **Figure 11.1** an example of the Marshmallow Challenge, bringing IT and business teams together in collaboration and teamwork.

Figure 11.1: The Marshmallow challenge

Along the way, I invested heavily in my own growth. I pursued advanced certifications — KMP (Kanban Management Professional), AKT (Accredited Kanban Trainer), SPC (SAFe Program Consultant), and CEC (Certified Enterprise Coach). Each milestone wasn't about collecting letters after my name but about sharpening my ability to guide others. These achievements gave me the privilege to certify and train colleagues, multiplying the impact across the company. Before long, IPC was recognized as one of the top Agile-certified companies in South Florida, not because of titles or credentials, but because of a culture of continuous learning and excellence.

Business Transformation Beyond IT

It sometimes felt like IPC had two different company cultures: IT and Business. My next challenge was to bridge that gap and extend Agile to the full organization.

Jan, our CEO, asked George to help expand the culture he had shaped within IT to the rest of the organization. George then came to me for support in leading that transition. As the transformation evolved, we introduced Agile principles beyond IT, helping business teams visualize their work, form cross-functional collaborations, and adopt practices like stand-ups and retrospectives **Figure 11.2** illustrates the collaboration. It was never about forcing Agile onto them but about guiding them with the same care and respect we had used with our tech teams.

Figure 11.2: Collaboration

When scaling, friction is inevitable. Leaders are asked to make trade-offs and work closer than they ever have before. During this period, tension grew between two organizational leaders. My CIO asked me to coach them. This was big for me, finally, a chance to address behavior issues that could shape unity across departments. But once I heard the names, I was torn. These were not just leaders, they were major influencers, and close friends. How could I navigate this?

I started by bringing them together, face to face. The intensity was palpable, like sitting between two storms colliding. Their eyes rarely met, and when they did, silence carried more weight than words. At first, the conversation skimmed the surface, circling symptoms instead of causes.

We had to dig deeper. Eventually, the truth surfaced: trust had been broken. Naming the real issue was the first step toward healing. I wish I could say challenges like this are resolved in one session, but they rarely are. Instead, we left with both leaders reflecting on small steps they could take to rebuild trust, knowing it would take time, effort, and commitment. As I sat with them, I felt the weight of my dual role as friend and coach. I didn't want to let either of them down. I knew they were stubborn, and this wouldn't be easy.

Part of me worried I didn't have all the tools I needed. But I reminded myself that listening without picking sides was the most powerful tool I had. Holding that tension required me to stay anchored in purpose: unity across the enterprise mattered more than my personal comfort. They never fully regained their old friendship, but they did something just as important, they found a way to work together again. They chose professionalism over pride, and that decision restored the trust the organization needed to move forward.

In November 2015, I trained the business in Kanban and coached them through their transformation. The support wasn't just classroom instruction, it included workshops to map and optimize workflows, and the creation of a Kanban board to visualize and improve the way work flowed.

We built cross-functional teams in co-located spaces within business units like Protein, Bakery, Beverage, and Snacks. These teams weren't cross-functional in name only, they took charge of end-to-end delivery, breaking down silos across Analysis,

Negotiation, Vendor Management, Logistics, and Quality. As the teams built their Kanban boards, it was inspiring to see them make the system their own. They showed pride in ensuring everything was visible and aligned, almost like they were hanging their values on the wall for everyone to see. Watching that filled me with pride too, it was validation that the spark had caught. That pride in ownership was a breakthrough moment for me as a coach; proof they were not just adopting a tool but embracing a mindset of transparency and accountability.

The results spoke for themselves. Protein teams cut vendor negotiation cycles by weeks. Bakery improved logistics planning, lowering costs and reducing delivery delays. Beverage unlocked new opportunities with faster cross-department collaboration, while Snacks developed innovative approaches to quality assurance. These weren't just process changes, they were proof that trust and empowerment drive measurable business outcomes.

It was a powerful moment of alignment. The principles that worked in IT proved equally effective across the business. That realization opened the door to true enterprise agility. I continued working with other departments, guiding them through transformations and helping them apply Agile principles in ways suited to their unique challenges.

One day, I was with several business units in a collaborative workshop. The energy was high, ideas flowing, conversations dynamic.

Then, an executive walked in. One of IPC's original founders. His presence shifted the room instantly. The air deflated like a punctured balloon. People held their breath. When he spoke, no one pushed back. Silence prevailed, not from agreement, but from fear.

Later, I was asked to hold sessions with him. During one, I shared my perspective on his leadership style and how others felt intimidated. He looked at me and said, "Good, that was my intention." I was shocked. On one hand, I appreciated his honesty. On the other, I didn't have a strong comeback. My chest tightened, thoughts raced, and for a moment I wondered if I was in over my head. He was sharp, and his intelligence made me question whether my approach would work. In that moment, I was caught off guard My genuine reaction in **Figure 11.3**.

Figure 11.3: He said what?

In that moment, I also recognized my own past in his words. As a Project Manager, I had been taught to lead in that very same way: commanding, decisive, leaving little room for alternative viewpoints. Back then, any suggestion of a different approach would have felt silly, unfounded, even weak. Hearing him say it so directly stirred up both empathy and vulnerability in me. I understood exactly where he was coming from, because I had once lived that mindset myself.

I tried a bit of reverse psychology, suggesting that perhaps it would be easier on him not to carry so much of the burden and risk burnout. He simply replied that in all his years, burnout had never been an issue for him.

It left me reflecting on a deeper question: how do you encourage someone to shift their leadership style when, by many external measures, they've been wildly successful?

In truth, it was hard to argue against the incredible success IPC had experienced under his leadership. But I also believed there was more potential to unlock, more creativity, collaboration, and shared ownership, if fear wasn't part of the equation.

To his credit, while he never fully embraced the Agile mindset, he didn't block the journey either. He allowed me to continue coaching his leadership team. That cautious openness gave us just enough momentum to keep moving forward. It wasn't a sweeping endorsement, but it was a quiet form of support that proved essential to sustaining the transformation.

These experiences taught me that enterprise coaching isn't just about scaling frameworks, it's about scaling belief, trust, and shared purpose. And in many ways, it mirrored my own personal journey: learning to let go of control, listen more deeply, and create space for others to thrive.

Key Learnings from Chapter 11

- Influence is earned through impact and integrity, not position or title.
- Unity grows when leaders have the courage to face conflict and rebuild trust.
- Psychological safety is the hidden engine of innovation, in the boardroom and at every team table.
- When teams take true ownership of practices like Kanban, process transforms into culture, and pride fuels progress.

When coaching becomes less about control and more about connection, real change begins. Frameworks help us align, but it's trust, context, and curiosity that move us forward. Scaling Agile isn't about pushing harder, it's about listening deeper, leading with purpose, and building bridges strong enough to carry everyone across.

Chapter 12:

Scaling Without Losing Culture

"If you want to go fast, go alone. If you want to go far, go together." — African Proverb

S caling Agile isn't about going bigger, it's about going deeper first. During this time, we also had a leadership transition. George began assisting in other executive areas, and Steven Elinson stepped in as our acting CIO. Steven is one of the most humble and approachable leaders I know. He had big shoes to fill, and he was up for the challenge. What made this moment special was that he opened the door for me to coach him and his executive team.

For me, this honor was not given, it was earned. Through collaborations with external companies and deep involvement in the community, I had the opportunity to build a program that was both meaningful and impactful for leaders.

Scaling Agile wasn't just another step, it was a whole new challenge. As an Enterprise Coach, I had to figure out how to grow what worked without losing what mattered. We needed to build structures that supported growth both horizontally and vertically, while still creating alignment and transparency across the organization. Steven's openness to coaching made this journey possible. His humility and willingness to engage in honest conversations with his executive team helped us anchor scaling efforts in trust and shared vision, rather than just process.

That leadership foundation gave us the confidence to experiment, learn, and adapt as we grew.

Even though Agile had spread throughout IT and into some business units, alignment issues persisted. Teams needed stronger collaboration, and more importantly, vertical alignment all the way up to executive leadership. To better understand what scaling required, I invested in learning the Scaled Agile Framework (SAFe), earning my SPC (SAFe Program Consultant) certification in late 2016.

We experimented with SAFe, but quickly realized a full implementation wasn't right for us. While it offered valuable tools and frameworks, applying it in its entirety felt too heavy and, at times, counterproductive. Instead, we took a pragmatic approach, adopting only the elements that fit our environment and goals. Culture had to remain our foundation.

> **Coaching Guidance:**
>
> There are many frameworks that can support Agile transformation, and each one offers useful tools depending on where a team or organization is in its maturity cycle. The key is to remain framework agnostic, don't get attached to one specific approach. What truly matters is how the practices support growth, build alignment, and help people take the next step forward in their journey. Frameworks are tools, not destinations. We need to keep the focus where it belongs: on people and outcomes.

One critical lesson we learned: don't scale dysfunction. If teams are misaligned, lacking trust, or unclear on their purpose, scaling only amplifies those problems. Before we could scale effectively, we had to make sure our teams were healthy, focused, and equipped to succeed. Scaling isn't just about structure; it's about knowing when the organization is truly ready. Without a strong foundation, even the best frameworks will collapse under pressure.

Big Room Planning: A Collaborative Approach

One of the most effective practices we adopted was Big Room Planning, a quarterly event that brought all teams together to align on work for the upcoming quarter. Steven's support was instrumental here, his presence and encouragement reassured teams that leadership was fully invested in both the process and the people.

Prerequisites:

A successful Big Room Planning session starts with leadership engagement and alignment. Leaders need a shared understanding of the Product Vision, Organizational Strategy, and High-Level Objectives, as well as a clear list of the top 10 priority initiatives. Working with leadership in this space wasn't always easy, I wasn't sure at first how the conversations would unfold or whether we would reach consensus. The workshops we held on strategy and vision became opportunities not just to clarify direction, but also to build trust and learn together.

Setting the Tone with Icebreakers

To kick things off, I led a high-energy Rock, Paper, Scissors icebreaker. Winners continued to compete while the others became their cheering section. The room buzzed with energy, reminding everyone that collaboration doesn't mean always getting your way, it means choosing to support one another. That small activity set the tone for the rest of the event.

Even executives joined in. Seeing them laugh, play, and then shift seamlessly into serious planning sent a powerful message: hierarchy would not stand in the way of teamwork. We also established clear working agreements that encouraged open dialogue and questions, ensuring no one held back.

Building a Shared Vision

The executive team's alignment stood out most. They articulated a shared vision with clarity and conviction, which grounded the planning process. Product Owners then presented top-priority features in order of value. Teams responded with sharp, thoughtful questions, showing they were fully engaged in shaping the work ahead.

Next, our technical leads walked everyone through the architectural runway. This wasn't just a technical overview; it was a chance to equip every team with the context they needed to make smart planning decisions. **Figure 12.1** shows the dynamic in the room to get consensus and alignment.

Figure 12.1: Fail to plan, plan to fail

Planning in Action

Then came the real magic. Teams mapped dependencies, identified risks, and forecasted their work for the quarter. The room came alive with movement and collaboration. Colorful stickers marked different workstreams, weaving together business features and the technical foundations to support them. We created a Program Board, as shown in **Figure 12.2.**

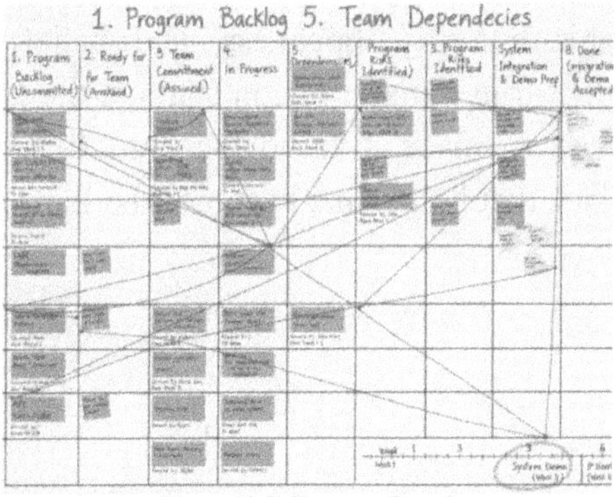

Figure 12.2: Program Board

The product board became the centerpiece, a massive chart showing every product and its connections. It was eye-opening. People suddenly saw how interconnected their work really was. Some were surprised, even shocked, to discover just how much their success depended on others. That moment reshaped how we thought about collaboration.

Leadership Alignment in Real Time

At the end of Day 1, the leadership team returned to review each plan. Their presence was intentional. They didn't just observe, they actively engaged, placing value points on the plans to reflect expected business impact. This practice gave us a quarterly feedback loop, where we could revisit and measure whether the value delivered matched the value anticipated. Unlike many companies, we weren't afraid to look back and learn, even at the executive level. That mindset accelerated trust across the organization.

In the end, scaling wasn't about processes or frameworks, it was about trust. It was about building a culture where people could align, adapt, and grow together. Steven's leadership reinforced that lesson, his humility, openness, and belief in coaching reminded us that true transformation starts at the top. And once that culture was in place, I faced the hardest decision of all, leaving the place that helped me become who I am.

Key Learnings from Chapter 12

- Scaling works only when teams are healthy and aligned; otherwise, dysfunction multiplies.
- Culture must remain the foundation as structures expand.
- Shared vision at the executive level is the anchor that keeps scaling real.
- True scaling is not just growth in numbers; it is deepening trust and alignment.

Scaling didn't mean letting go of who we were, it meant holding on tighter to what mattered most. The frameworks helped us organize, but it was trust, clarity, and connection that kept us human. Growth without soul isn't transformation, it's just expansion. The real challenge was never scaling Agile, it was scaling care, purpose, and belief in each other.

Chapter 13:

Leaving, but Not Letting Go

The hardest part of growth? Leaving the place that helped you become who you are. In 2018, I made the difficult decision to leave IPC. It wasn't just a job, it was home. As I walked out of that building for the last time, a wave of gratitude, pride, and sadness washed over me. IPC had been more than a workplace; it had become a part of who I was. I had grown more there, personally and professionally, than in any other role. I entered IPC as a Project Manager and left as a leader shaped by purpose and people. I had become someone I barely recognized, in the best way possible.

But I also knew it was time to take what I'd learned and share it with the world.

Rick's Keynote Session

My final act before leaving IPC was standing on a stage at NextEra, one of the largest employers in Florida, delivering a keynote titled "Stepping Out of Your Comfort Zone" (see me back then in **Figure 13.1**).The title couldn't have been more symbolic. It reflected not just a professional transition, but a personal leap into a future shaped by everything IPC had taught me.

Figure 13.1: Rick's keynote session

I shared the IPC journey as a case study of cultural and organizational change, highlighting the lessons that shaped me and the impact that transformation can have when rooted in trust, empowerment, and purpose. It was a full-circle moment—honoring where I had come from as I stepped into something new.

As I prepared for that keynote, I couldn't help but reflect on how much life had changed since the day I joined IPC. The person standing on that stage wasn't the same man who had once walked into those halls uncertain of what kind of leader he wanted to be. The road between those two moments was filled with challenges that tested my limits and victories that redefined my understanding of success.

And somewhere along that journey, somewhere between the exhaustion, the breakthroughs, and the rediscovery of purpose, I met Regina.

Meeting the love of my life

At the time, I was serving as VP of Membership for the South Florida PMI Chapter, responsible for engaging professionals who might want to join our community. One afternoon, I invited a young woman named Regina Batista, a PMO Manager from the building across from IPC, to attend one of our events. From the moment we met, I was struck by her presence—intelligent, confident, and full of grace. Something about her energy was grounding and electric at the same time.

I'll admit, I was nervous and wanted to make a good impression. When I get nervous, I tend to talk a lot, so I decided to take her on a tour of IPC's Agile team spaces and share the story of our transformation. Every hallway conversation made me feel more alive. When she left, I knew I wanted to talk to her again. After a few moments of hesitation, I took a deep breath and sent her a text with one word: "Cute". It took her a while to respond. Finally, she wrote, "I think you might have made a mistake sending this text." I smiled and replied, "I don't make that kind of mistake."

That brief exchange felt playful and daring, the kind of moment that changes everything.

That small act of courage led me to the love of my life. Regina became my balance, my sounding board, my inspiration, and my partner in every sense. She saw me not for the titles or achievements, but for the person behind them. Her strength, kindness, and belief in me mirrored the same principles that had defined our transformation at IPC, trust, empathy, and courage.

Together, we grew not just as partners but as leaders, learning to balance ambition with care and success with purpose. Her perspective grounded me. Her faith in me pushed me forward. And her love gave me the courage to believe that the work I was doing mattered beyond any title or recognition. **Figure 13.2** captured us in our early days.

Figure 13.2: Rick and Regina

A Proposal to Remember

That same day, during my keynote at NextEra, I decided to take the biggest leap of all, I asked Regina to marry me. I knew it couldn't be ordinary. It had to reflect who we were: creative, passionate, and a little unpredictable.

With the full blessing of her boss and the event's executive sponsor, I secretly planned to propose on stage. As the conference came to a close, we were wrapping up a discussion on Agile leadership with the NextEra leadership team. I turned to the audience and said I wanted to end with a short exercise about visualizing your future and the power of projecting your vision.

You can see the video in the link down below:

With hundreds of people watching, I invited Regina on stage to help me. She smiled, unaware of what was about to happen. I handed her a paper bag and asked her to open an empty box, pretending it was a symbolic "gift of the future." But instead of an empty box, there was a ring inside.

For a moment, time froze. The crowd went silent. As she opened the box, realization washed over her face. I dropped to one knee and asked her to marry me. Everything after that felt like slow motion, the applause, the laughter, her stunned expression.

Watching the video later, I realized I stayed on one knee far longer than I remembered. Regina was so shocked that she kept saying, "No, no, no!" For a split second, my heart stopped, wondering if she meant it. Then someone from the audience called out, "Did you say yes?" and she laughed through her tears, saying, "Yes! I said yes!"

The room erupted in cheers. In that moment, surrounded by hundreds of people, I realized that the same courage that once helped me send that first text had just changed my life again.

Transformation Experts

A new chapter began when I partnered with Regina to co-found Transformation Experts, an Agile Transformation Consulting firm dedicated to helping organizations evolve with empathy, empowerment, and purpose. See **Figure 13.3** that showcases the unity between Rick and Regina on Transformation Experts first days. This wasn't about recreating IPC, it was about applying everything IPC had taught me and building a space where others could experience their own transformation.

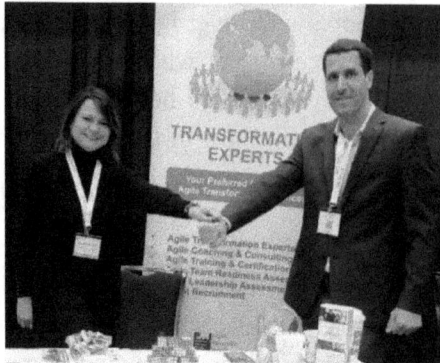

Figure 13.3: From IPC lessons to building Transformation Experts.

The road wasn't easy. Starting a company meant facing new challenges: building credibility, creating structure, balancing vision with execution. But just like before, it wasn't the obstacles that defined the journey, it was the people, the lessons, and the belief that culture always comes first.

Since then, I've had the privilege of guiding leaders, teams, and entire organizations through their own journeys, always remembering the lessons from that Kanban board, that data center, that gratitude tree, and that incredible team who taught me what's possible when culture meets courage.

I'll never forget IPC: the people, the growth, the purpose. It's the closest I've ever seen to true transformation. George Labelle's courage. Steven Elinson's integrity. Christina Alonso's joyful mentorship. Bob Sarnak's conviction. Each of them shaped the leader I am today.

Even as I stepped into new organizations, part of IPC always came with me in the way I coached, in the culture I cultivated, and in the belief that real change starts with people.

Leaving IPC wasn't the end of my Agile journey; it was the beginning of my mission to help others discover that real change is possible. The journey didn't just transform my teams; it transformed me as a leader. It became a path of discovery, revealing who I was meant to be and how I was meant to lead.

And now, I was ready to pass it on.

Key Learnings from Chapter 13

- Growth sometimes requires leaving a place you love.
- The impact of a workplace lives on in the leaders and lessons it shapes.
- Sharing your story can inspire others to take bold steps of their own.
- The journey of discovery doesn't end when you leave an organization; it continues in who you become and how you lead.

Leaving wasn't the end of the story. It was the moment I realized the story was mine to carry forward. I didn't leave because it stopped mattering, I left because it mattered so much, I couldn't ignore the pull to do more. The lessons, the people, the transformation, they became part of me. And as I stepped into the unknown, I wasn't walking away. I was walking with purpose; toward the next chapter I hadn't yet written.

Conclusion:

This Was Never Just About Agile

Transformation isn't a buzzword, it's a battle. One that's deeply personal, painfully honest, and profoundly human. Looking back, this journey wasn't about Agile frameworks or sticky notes on whiteboards. It was about people, scared, curious, hopeful people, willing to try something new. Willing to believe that work could feel different. That leadership could be about empathy, not ego. That teams could be built on trust instead of fear.

It was about unlearning the habits that once helped us survive but were now holding us back.

At IPC, I witnessed something rare: a culture that didn't just tolerate change, it embraced it. We questioned everything. We opened our doors to the world. We chose transparency over polish, courage over comfort, and people over process. And because of that, we didn't just evolve, we inspired.

But the real message isn't what we built at IPC. It's that this kind of transformation is possible anywhere, if you're willing to do the hard work. If you're willing to listen. To let go. To grow.

I wrote this book because I believe more leaders need to hear that it's okay to feel stuck, and it's possible to change. I wrote it for the burned-out Project manager who doesn't recognize themselves anymore. For the executive who wonders why their teams aren't engaged. For the new hire who dreams of a culture where they can actually thrive.

This journey of leadership discovery reshaped my life. Not because of any single ceremony or practice, but because it reminded me of who I was and revealed who I could become as a leader.

That's the legacy of IPC. And it's the heartbeat of everything I do now.

So wherever you are in your journey, whether you're starting out, leading change, or just trying to hold it all together, I hope this story reminds you: you're not alone. Transformation is messy, imperfect, and slow... until it's not. And when it finally takes hold, it can shift everything.

The question is no longer, "Can we change?"
It's "Will we choose to?"

And if we do, what might we discover about ourselves, our teams, and the leaders we are capable of becoming?

Different points of view:

I recently had a conversation with someone who lived through the Agile transformation I write about in my book.
Hearing their perspective was eye-opening.

One of my biggest lessons has been realizing how easy it is to be biased toward your own point of view. We often mistake our experiences for absolute reality, forgetting that what we see is only one side of the truth. A single viewpoint offers just a partial reflection.

It's not until we open ourselves to conversations with others, especially those who feel safe enough to speak honestly without fear of judgment, that we begin to see other angles of what really happened. Those perspectives can shift our understanding in powerful ways.

This ties back to the importance of setting clear expectations and remembering that spoken and written language is imperfect. Words can be misinterpreted. Meanings can drift over time. Even our own messages can lose clarity. That's why communication needs to be revisited often, to ensure understanding is not just intended but achieved.

Communication is never one-sided. It's a two-way exchange built on curiosity, listening, and a willingness to see beyond ourselves.

In leadership and in life, real growth begins when we choose to see through someone else's eyes.

Voices from the Journey

George Labelle, CIO (Retired), IPC:

"Six months after deciding to abandon IPC's waterfall methodology and move the entire organization to Agile, I often lay awake at night filled with doubt. Projects had been late, over budget, and frequently obsolete before completion. Our business partners were frustrated, outsourcing work, and I knew my job was at risk if I didn't find a better way. At a Gartner conference I discovered Agile, and the very next Monday I told my team, 'We are going Agile, starting now.' Some thought I'd gone mad. Looking back, I'm grateful we stayed the course. Agile reshaped how we delivered, how we led, and how we connected. It changed a company, a culture, and a life, mine. And one of the most important influences along the way was Rick Regueira, whose guidance helped me navigate the uncertainty and grow through the experience."

Steven Elinson Acting CIO:

"Rick's leadership created a culture where experimentation, failure, and learning drove continuous growth. By empowering teams to embrace healthy conflict and hold each other accountable, he transformed challenges into opportunities for trust and collaboration. His guidance showed that TRUE empowerment is born not from avoiding mistakes, but from confronting them openly, learning together, and growing stronger through shared accountability and resilience."

Daniel Silva, VP3 Lead Developer:

"Transitioning from a traditional waterfall model to an agile scrum methodology was a transformative experience. The shift to using physical boards, breaking down work into manageable sprints, and empowering our engineering teams significantly enhanced our focus and accelerated business delivery. By enabling engineers to apply test-driven development and invest in automated testing upfront, we not only increased the quality of our output but also made downstream implementation simpler and more cost-effective. This new approach built a deep sense of trust, gave us a lot of agency, and maximized value for the entire organization. I'm so grateful for this experience; it forever imprinted on me a way of working that has greatly improved my productivity."

Jason Ertel,VP3 Developer:

"I never considered Agile to be the key that unlocked our success at VP3. I believe it was having enough key players with the right attitude, experience, confidence, humility, and work ethic that drove the success of the projects. I believe having enough high output key players on a team is enough to make most projects, and teams, successful. Perhaps Agile is owed some credit in that it prevented outside forces from interfering with those key players' planning and time. It is also possible that when enough of the team already believes in some of the same underlying principles of Agile (respect, listening to each other; being there for each other), overlaying Agile onto the team doesn't produce a significant divergence from the original team's attributes, but rather is an additive formula, where the difference can be summarized as stickies, standups, and retrospectives. On that note, the one property of Agile that I've carried forward with me is the standup meeting procedure: going around the room (or call) with a brief summary from each team member, and following that with deeper discussions on tagged topics with those team members interested that topic"

Andre Spaulding Global Logistics Manager:

"At the Independent Purchasing Cooperative (Subway Coop), I served as the Global Logistics Manager for North America, responsible for creating procurement, distribution, and logistics strategies to support the movement of a $4.5 billion spend. When I first joined, the teams operated in a highly fragmented manner, but under the leadership, guidance, and patience of Rick Regueira, who introduced the Agile methodology, I helped drive the transition from siloed functions to fully integrated cross-functional teams. This shift enabled us to implement more optimal, technology-driven solutions that delivered measurable savings for Subway franchisees both domestically and internationally. By applying Agile principles, I contributed to transforming Subway's supply chain from rudimentary practices into one of the most robust in the QSR industry, so much so that it was often said Subway had become an IT company that made great sandwiches, rather than just a sandwich company."

Bob Sarnack, Quality Control Analyst:

"I was hired on at IPC as a Quality Control Analyst, a tester. I was the tester for all Software Development. All of my tests were run manually. After I arrived, I started working with the development teams to create an automated test suite to ensure that no errors were being introduced into Production. After the changes requested by our Product Owners were migrated to the Preproduction environment the automated tests were run. The test suite was run as the code for each User Story was complete and checked into the Preproduction environment. If errors were encountered, the check-in was backed out of Preproduction and the test suite run again to ensure that no unforeseen errors still existed.

As the automated test suite matured, I was able to change my focus from manually testing to providing the Developers with the tests I was going to run for each User Story. These tests now became part of the User Story and became part of the User Story acceptance criteria. A Story could not be added to an Iteration unless it had these tests. Now the developers could include migrating the tests to the automated test suite when they migrated their code to the Preproduction environment. This led to the teams transitioning to TDD.

As the developers became comfortable with the tests I was going to include as part of the User Story, some began to take on the QC role of each team. This allowed me to transition from my Quality Control role to more of a Quality Assurance role. Where QC focuses on the end product or service, QA focuses on the processes that are used to deliver that product or service. I was still aware of errors that were encountered, so I now focused on the processes that allowed those errors to get to the Preproduction environment and how those processes needed to be improved.

I could see how Agile Software Development is process focused and it seemed natural to me to start transitioning my role to be a Scrum Master. As a Quality Manager I fully embraced the Agile model of software development. It is structured yet flexible. It is focused on delivering quality value to the customer. After a short period of time, I became a certified Scrum Master and was assigned to be the Scrum Master for a couple of teams. Other certifications followed, such as becoming SAFE certified.

At IPC we formed the Scrum Masters as an independent sub-team. We met regularly and discussed how we could help contribute to make our teams more high performing and how we could help each other with the challenges we were facing. I remember one Scrum Master was a member of five teams. That was unacceptable to us, as they could not give each team the guidance that they deserved. So, one of us became the new Scrum Master of one of the teams. That helped the team and the Scrum Master.

One characteristic of Agile teams is that they are self-organizing. The previous is one example of self-organizing teams. The degree of self-organization can vary with each team. One of my most memorable examples of a highly self-organized team is as follows: It was coming up on performance review time, where each individual is reviewed for their previous year's performance and the monetary benefits associated with that performance. We as a team, told leadership that we deliver quality value as a team, you will review us as a team. And George, the great leader he is, agreed with this, and we were reviewed as a team. That blew me away. I had never experienced anything like that in my previous places of employment."

Marcelo Lopez, Agile Coach:

I wasn't sure what or how to put into words what I wanted to say here. When you've lived, laughed, cried (yeah, cried), struggled, challenged and overcome things together, trying to pull at any given thread of that experience is difficult to do. That's because if you take 3 steps back from looking at your experiences together closely, what you find is that you've woven a tapestry out of life together with that person. I've known Rick for almost 2 decades now. I've been there for most of the "journey of discovery". Back in 2012, we both decided to become Scrum Alliance Guides at the same time. He pursued his CEC, while I my CST. We decided to put our experience with Kanban to good use to become the 3rd and 4th Spanish-speaking AKT's (It doesn't matter who was 3rd and who was 4th, but 'L' DOES come before 'R" in the alphabet) over a decade ago.

We've traveled for work together (gotten stuck in SNOW together). We've traveled for community together (what's up Agile Florida!). And oh yes, from the very beginning when Rick decided to form the South Florida Agile Association with some of our local community friends, we were in it to win it. Since then, he and I have shared the stage at conferences as speakers trading off ideas of what made our teams and management endeavors WORK (and what didn't work so well). Moreover, after so many years and in-person meetups, he took on the challenge to take us "full remote" at the start of the pandemic, and within 2 months had our first fully remote conference up and running. We had over 150 attendees from around the world that day. Since then, we've had thousands of visitors join us almost weekly, representing nearly 100 countries. So, the title of this book is apropos because it absolutely has been a journey of discovery.

Community. Leadership by showing up again and again and again. Being present for ANYONE and everyone who came hungry with questions and concerns and just wanted to be heard. That's leadership.

Thanks for the memories past, and those to come, Rick. Congratulations, and here's to what's ahead for you in the future, my friend. The road to the stars is hard. Liftoff!

About the author:

Rick Regueira
Executive Agile Coach
CEC, AKT, SPC6, PMP

Rick Regueira is an Enterprise Agile Coach, author, keynote speaker, and founder of Transformation Experts. With more than 20 years of experience in IT and business transformation, he has guided Fortune 500 companies and executive leaders through cultural shifts that create lasting impact. His work centers on building high-performing teams and organizations rooted in trust, empathy, and continuous improvement.

Rick's career has been defined by helping leaders and teams embrace change, break down silos, and unlock their full potential. He has led large-scale Agile transformations, designed leadership development programs, and created thriving professional communities that continue to inspire growth and connection worldwide.

Passionate about the intersection of Agile and AI, Rick helps organizations harness technology while keeping people at the center. As a dynamic speaker and coach, he brings real-world stories, practical tools, and a deep belief that true transformation begins with people. His mission is simple: to help others discover that change is not only possible, but powerful.

About Transformation Experts

Transformation Experts is an Agile transformation and leadership development company dedicated to helping organizations unlock their potential. We partner with executives, leaders, and teams to create environments where people thrive, businesses adapt, and innovation grows.

- Agile Coaching & Training
- Executive & Leadership Coaching
- Strategic Workshops & Keynotes
- AI & Digital Transformation Consulting
- Career Development & Agile Talent Programs

Let's Connect

✉ Email: rick.regueira@te-culture.com

∞ LinkedIn: https://www.linkedin.com/in/rickregueira

TRANSFORMATION
EXPERTS

Transformation
Expertes Website

www.teculture.com

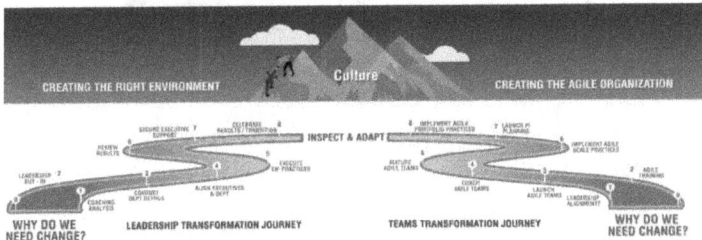

FREE Agile International Coaching Meetups!

Each week, Transformation Experts hosts the Agile International Coaching Clinic, a free space for professionals to connect, ask questions, and grow together. Facilitated by some of the top coaches and trainers in the industry. Marcelo Lopez, Arthur Zigman, Regina Batista, Joseph Labara, Taz Brown, Leon Sabarsky.

Transformation
Expertes Free
Events

www.teculture.com/free-events

Special Thanks

A heartfelt thank you to the incredible coaches and volunteers who have supported the Agile International Coaching Meetups and contributed to the growth of this global community. Your passion, dedication, and generosity continue to inspire and elevate others on their leadership journeys.

Special recognition to: Tina Ahonle, Sabah Benson, Julie Bruton, Joane Aristilde, Rolando Segovia, Viral Barot, Jackie Beckford, Karen Kureshi, Andre Noudjo, Syed Sharafat Ali, and Carol Casas. Your time, energy, and commitment have made an unforgettable impact.

Nothing would be possible without the back-office team who keeps us afloat. Jesus Cabrera, Josuel Diaz, Aly Simbulan, and Kaye Nocillado.

Book Rick to Speak:

Rick Regueira is the CEO of Transformation Experts, President of the South Florida Agile Association, and a global keynote speaker who has shared his message at events across North America, Latin America, Europe, and Asia.

His talks blend storytelling, practical insights, and emotional intelligence to help leaders and teams rediscover what truly drives performance, connection, courage, and culture.

"Agile isn't just a framework, it's a way to unlock human potential."

Rick's speaking
landing page

☐www.teculture.com/rick-regueira

Speaking Topics:

- Executive Coaching
- Organizational Transformation
- AI for High Performing Teams
- A Leadership Journey of Discovery
- Overcoming Adversity

Key Milestones in IPC's Organizational Transformation

1. Leadership Commitment to Change (2010)

- **CIO George Labelle** declares the move to Agile after recognizing the limits of traditional project management.
- Marks the official **start of IPC's enterprise transformation journey** — leadership-driven, not process-driven.

2. Organization-Wide Agile Training

- Mandatory two-day Agile training for all technology employees led by **Angela Johnson**.
- Established a **shared language of values and principles**, shifting focus from "managing projects" to **empowering people**.

3. Cultural and Structural Reset

- Executives **give up private offices**, and cubicle walls come down to foster collaboration.
- Introduction of new core values:
  Franchisee Focus – Humble Professional – Make Things Happen.
- The first visible **alignment of environment and behavior** with Agile values.

4. Formation of Cross-Functional Agile Teams

- Technology reorganized into **small, empowered teams** (7–9 members).
- **Scrum Master** and **Product Owner** roles created.
- Shared services (Infrastructure, Security, DB) integrated into team ceremonies.
  Silos begin to dissolve; **horizontal collaboration replaces departmental control.**

5. Infrastructure Transformation via Kanban (2011–2012)

- The infrastructure team adopts **Kanban** to visualize work, limit WIP, and improve flow.
- Results in major performance and trust improvements.
- **Recognized by Gartner** as an example of practical Agile implementation in infrastructure.

6. Emergence of High-Performing Teams (2012–2013)

- VP3 Credit Card Processing team becomes the **model of Agile excellence:**
  - Peer-selected leadership.
  - Continuous integration and automation.
  - Team-based performance reviews.
- Establishes **psychological safety and shared accountability** as organizational norms.

7. Community Expansion and Thought Leadership (2013–2014)

- Creation of **South Florida Agile Association (SFAA)** and the **High-Performing Teams Conference (HPTC)** hosted at IPC.
- Agile principles move beyond IPC's walls — **community becomes a multiplier of transformation.**
- CEO **Jan Risi** publicly endorses Agile at the conference closing keynote.

8. Launch of the IPC Executive Agile Experience (2014–2016)

- Quarterly immersive program inviting **vendors and executives from other companies** to witness Agile in action.
- Over **80 organizations** hosted; IPC recognized as a **benchmark for cultural transformation.**
- Awards earned:
  - *CIO 100 Award*
  - *Computerworld Best Places to Work (#16)*
  - *QSR Applied Technology Award*
  - *Hospitality Technology Edge Award.*

9. Agile Coaching and Organizational Restructuring (2015–2016)

- Formation of **Agile Coaching Chapter** to develop and mentor Scrum Masters.
- Employee-led **organizational redesign** based on empowerment and transparency.

- Tools and models used: Belbin, Five Dysfunctions, Tribal Leadership.
- Transformation shifts from *Agile adoption* to *Agile culture ownership*.

10. Expansion Beyond IT – Business Agility (2016)

- Agile extended into **business units** (Protein, Bakery, Beverage, Snacks).
- Creation of **cross-functional business teams** with end-to-end accountability.
- Outcomes:
  - Faster vendor negotiation cycles.
  - Improved logistics and delivery efficiency.
  - Greater collaboration between business and IT.

11. Scaling Agile Across the Enterprise (2016–2017)

- **Steven Elinson** (acting CIO) introduces **Big Room Planning** and scaled collaboration events.
- Partial **SAFe adoption**, customized to IPC's culture.
- Enterprise alignment achieved through shared vision, transparency, and strategy execution.
- Scaling focused on **trust before the process**, avoiding "mechanical Agile."

12. Sustained Agility and Legacy (2017–2018)

- IPC becomes one of the **most Agile-certified organizations in South Florida.**
- Culture of empathy, empowerment, and experimentation embedded company-wide.
- Transformation evolves from a project to a **way of working and leading.**

Milestone	Year(s)	Transformation Outcome
Leadership commitment	2010	Agile vision declared; top-down sponsorship
Company-wide Agile training	2010	Shared principles and language established
Cultural reset	2010– 2011	Core values, open spaces, collaboration
Cross-functional teams	2011	Structural alignment with Agile values
Kanban in Infrastructure	2011– 2012	Flow, trust, and visibility achieved
High-performing teams	2012– 2013	Culture of ownership and psychological safety
Community & HPTC	2013– 2014	External influence, internal pride
Executive Agile Experience	2014– 2016	National recognition and replication
Agile Coaching Chapter	2015– 2016	Self-organizing organizational structure
Business Agility	2016	Agile expands beyond IT to core business
Enterprise Scaling	2016– 2017	Big Room Planning, SAFe adaptation
Sustained Agility	2017– 2018	IPC becomes culture-first, adaptive enterprise

Special Acknowledgments:

I want to honor those who played central roles in shaping this journey, individuals whose stories and contributions appear throughout this book: George Labelle, Angela Johnson, Tony Ronconi, Bob Sarnack, Jason Ertel, Ariel Alonso, Marcelo Lopez, James Grenning, Jan Risi, Steven Elinson, Sion Dinh, Kelly-Ann Pinnock, Christina Alonso, Daniel Silva, Fernando Mejia, Andre Spaulding, Cindy Roge, Tito Guardado, Evan Williams and Mark Henschel. Their leadership, insight, and dedication left an indelible mark on our path.

Many others also contributed in meaningful ways, and their impact is deeply appreciated, even if not named here.

Among those whose influence I would like to highlight:

Stephanie Sylvestre is an amazing person who showed me what a servant leader truly looks like. She carried herself with no ego or animosity, only humility and care. Every time I needed help, she was there, supportive, giving, and authentic. Stephanie is a caring leader, and I am grateful for the example she set.

Abe (Abraham Fathman) is someone I met early in my journey and who has stood out ever since. His technical skills are exceptional, but what sets him apart is his understanding of culture. Where most developers focus only on code, Abe brought connection, empathy, and a coaching mindset. His ability to communicate and inspire made it clear that great software is as much about people as it is about technology. I remain grateful for his insight and friendship.

Tito Guardado: In every company, there's that one person everyone gravitates toward, the one with a ready smile, humble spirit, and contagious optimism. For us, that was Tito. A key member of the support team, he connected easily with everyone, from the CEO to frontline staff. His go-lucky nature made workdays lighter, and his laughter and positivity lifted everyone around him. Professional and empathetic, Tito bridged business and IT, building trust through patience and clear communication. When projects hit rough patches, he was the calm voice that steadied conversations, managed expectations, and preserved relationships. People like Tito remind us that flow isn't just about moving tasks; it's about the people who keep trust and collaboration alive when challenges arise.

I am deeply grateful to the IPC Agile Team, who embraced change, brought our values to life, and turned vision into reality. To our community team, who carried that spirit beyond IPC's walls, expanding Agile knowledge worldwide, you inspired a movement that continues to grow.

To all who walked beside me and at times carried me forward, thank you. This book is as much yours as it is mine.

Index